O9-ABG-607

INVENTORS WHO CHANGED THE WORLD

ALEXANDER GRAHAM BELL

THE GENIUS BEHIND THE PHONE

STEPHEN FEINSTEIN

MyReportLinks.com Books

an imprint of

Enslow Publishers, Inc.

Box 398, 40 Industrial Road
Berkeley Heights, NJ 07922
USA

MyReportLinks.com Books, an imprint of Enslow Publishers, Inc. MyReportLinks®
is a registered trademark of Enslow Publishers, Inc.

Library of Congress Cataloging-in-Publication Data

Feinstein, Stephen.
  Alexander Graham Bell : the genius behind the phone / Stephen Feinstein.
      p. cm. — (Inventors who changed the world)
  Includes bibliographical references and index.
  ISBN-13: 978-1-59845-055-2 (hardcover : alk. paper)
  ISBN-10: 1-59845-055-7 (hardcover : alk. paper)
  1. Bell, Alexander Graham, 1847–1922—Juvenile literature. 2. Inventors—United States—
Biography—Juvenile literature. 3. Telephone—United States—History—Juvenile literature. I. Title.
  TK6143.B4F46 2007
  621.385092—dc22
  [B]
                                      2006033891

Printed in the United States of America

10 9 8 7 6 5 4 3 2 1

To Our Readers:
Through the purchase of this book, you and your library gain access to the Report Links that specifically
back up this book.
The Publisher will provide access to the Report Links that back up this book and will keep these Report
Links up to date on **www.myreportlinks.com** for five years from the book's first publication date.
We have done our best to make sure all Internet addresses in this book were active and appropriate when
we went to press. However, the author and the Publisher have no control over, and assume no liability
for, the material available on those Internet sites or on other Web sites they may link to.
The usage of the MyReportLinks.com Books Web site is subject to the terms and conditions stated on the
Usage Policy Statement on **www.myreportlinks.com.**
A password may be required to access the Report Links that back up this book. The password is found
on the bottom of page 4 of this book.
Any comments or suggestions can be sent by e-mail to comments@myreportlinks.com or to the address
on the back cover.

Photo Credits: The Alexander Graham Bell Papers at the Library of Congress, pp. 32, 96, 108, 109;
The Alexander Graham Bell Family Papers, Library of Congress, pp. 52, 53, 67, 69, 71; Gilbert
H. Grosvenor Collection, Prints and Photographs Division, Library of Congress, pp. 5, 22; Gilbert
H. Grosvenor Collection of Photographs of the Alexander Graham Bell Family, Library of Congress,
pp. 23, 30, 47, 84, 91, 113; The Image Works, pp. 1, 3; Library of Congress, pp. 39, 50;
MyReportLinks.com Books, p. 4; The National Archives and Records Administration, pp. 75, 77;
© Photos.com, p. 1; Prints and Photographs Division, Library of Congress, pp. 38, 58, 104, 105;
ShutterStock, pp. 8, 20, 40, 56, 82, 94; VelocityStock, p. 85.

Cover Photo: Bell, © Photos.com; image of first phone, The Image Works

CONTENTS

About MyReportLinks.com Books.   4

Important Dates   6

**1 COMMUNICATION BEFORE THE
INVENTION OF THE TELEPHONE**   8

**2 ALEXANDER GRAHAM BELL:
THE EARLY YEARS** 20

3 EXPERIMENTS WITH TELEGRAPHY . . . 40

4 INVENTING THE TELEPHONE 56

**5 HOW THE TELEPHONE CHANGED
THE WORLD** 82

6 BELL'S OTHER INVENTIONS 94

A Telecommunications Experiment. . . . 114

Report Links. 118

Glossary. 120

Chapter Notes. 122

Further Reading. 125

Index 126

MyReportLinks.com Books
Great Books, Great Links, Great for Research!

The Internet sites featured in this book can save you hours of research time. These Internet sites—we call them *"Report Links"*—are constantly changing, but we keep them up to date on our Web site.

When you see this "Approved Web Site" logo, you will know that we are directing you to a great Internet site that will help you with your research.

Give it a try! Type http://www.myreportlinks.com into your browser, click on the series title and enter the password, then click on the book title, and scroll down to the Report Links listed for this book.

The Report Links will bring you to great source documents, photographs, and illustrations. MyReportLinks.com Books save you time, feature Report Links that are kept up to date, and make report writing easier than ever! A complete listing of the Report Links can be found on pages 118–119 at the back of the book.

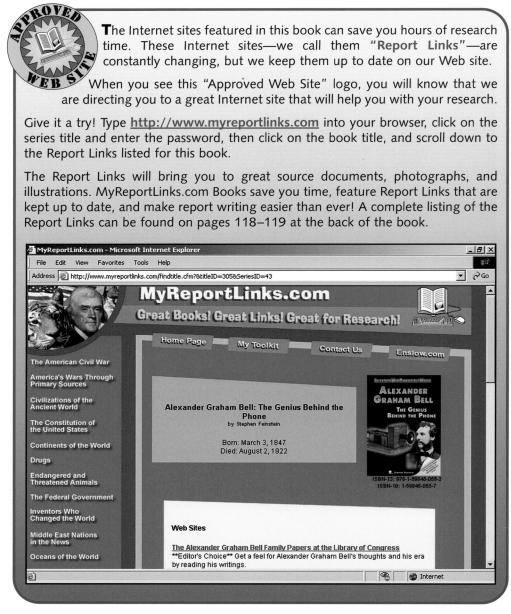

Please see "To Our Readers" on the copyright page for important information about this book, the MyReportLinks.com Web site, and the Report Links that back up this book.

Please enter AGB1473 if asked for a password.

Leave the beaten track occasionally and dive into the woods. Every time you do so you will be certain to find something that you have never seen before.

—Alexander Graham Bell

Important Dates

1847—Alexander Graham Bell is born on March 3 in Edinburgh, Scotland.

1862—Travels to live with his grandfather for a year in London.

1863—Accepts a teaching position in Elgin, Scotland.

1868—Teaches at the London School for the Deaf, where he uses his father's Visible Speech system.

1870—Emigrates to Canada with his parents.

1871—Begins teaching at the Boston School for Deaf-Mutes in April.

1874—Invents an improved phonautograph.

1875—The Bell Patent Association is formed. Bell transmits the first notes over a telephone on June 2.

1876—Receives the first patent for a telephone on March 7. On March 10, Bell speaks the first words ever heard over the telephone. On June 25, Bell demonstrates his telephone at the Centennial Exhibition in Philadelphia and wins the Grand Prize.

1877—Bell and his partners form the Bell Telephone Company. Bell marries Mabel Hubbard on July 11.

1879—Invents the audiometer and the bel unit that measures loudness.

1880—Invents the photophone.

1881—Invents the metal detector and the vacuum jacket respirator.

1898—After his father-in law's death in 1897, Bell inherits responsibility for the National Geographic Society, becoming its second president. In 1903, he appoints Gilbert H. Grosvenor, his son-in-law, to edit the society's magazine,

National Geographic. Grosvenor's addition of photographs to the magazine attracts millions of readers.

1907—Bell and partners form the Aerial Experiment Association to develop manned flight.

1909—Bell's *Silver Dart* makes the first engine-powered manned flight in Canada.

1911—Builds the HD-1, his first hydrofoil boat.

1915—Bell and Thomas Watson have first coast-to-coast telephone conversation on January 25.

1919—Bell's HD-4 hydrofoil boat sets a world speed record of 71 miles per hour (114 kilometers per hour).

1922—Bell dies at Beinn Bhreagh, Nova Scotia, on August 2.

COMMUNICATION BEFORE THE INVENTION OF THE TELEPHONE

Imagine what the world was like before the telephone was invented. To speak to a neighbor or somebody who lived on another street or in another part of town, it was necessary to go and visit the person. People had to write letters to keep in touch with friends or relatives who lived far away. Today, we take modern telecommunications for granted. Most people rarely take the time or trouble to write a letter—we send e-mails instead. As for the telephone, it seems as if almost every person owns a cell phone and uses it most of the time. It is difficult for us in the twenty-first century to imagine a time when people did not have such instant access to other people or to news from around the world.

Chapter 1

PROBLEMS CAUSED BY SLOW COMMUNICATION

By today's standards, communication in the old days was very slow. People were used to it, so it often was not a problem. But the delay in communicating important information sometimes had very serious consequences. News of major events or developments traveled slowly. News had to be carried by horse, train, ship, or on foot.

Transatlantic communication could take weeks, even months. On December 24, 1814, negotiators signed a peace treaty in Belgium that ended the War of 1812 between the United States and Great Britain. On January 2, 1815, the negotiators boarded a ship in London, England, to carry the news of the war's end to the United States. Unfortunately, the ship ran into bad weather and did not reach the United States until February 11.

Meanwhile, on January 8, 1815, American troops under the command of General Andrew Jackson held off a British assault on the city of New Orleans. The British forces suffered more than 2,000 casualties, while 71 American troops were killed or wounded. The Battle of New Orleans took place after the war ended, because the American and British generals had not yet learned that the war was over. If telephones, or even the transatlantic telegraph, had been invented by this time, it is quite possible that none of those British or American troops would have been hurt or killed.

⇒ The Invention of the Telegraph

Less than thirty years after the War of 1812 ended, the ability to communicate quickly over long distances had improved dramatically.

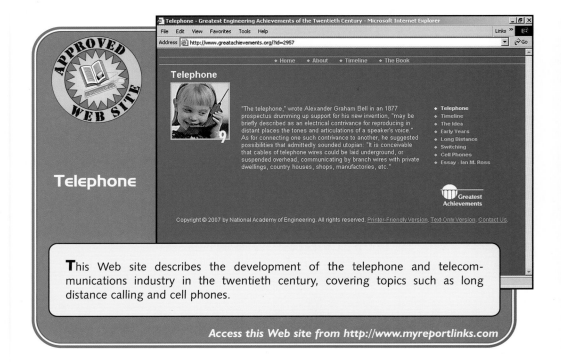

Telephone

"The telephone," wrote Alexander Graham Bell in an 1877 prospectus drumming up support for his new invention, "may be briefly described as an electrical contrivance for reproducing in distant places the tones and articulations of a speaker's voice." As for connecting one such contrivance to another, he suggested possibilities that admittedly sounded utopian: "It is conceivable that cables of telephone wires could be laid underground, or suspended overhead, communicating by branch wires with private dwellings, country houses, shops, manufactories, etc."

Telephone

◆ Telephone
◆ Timeline
◆ The Idea
◆ Early Years
◆ Long Distance
◆ Switching
◆ Cell Phones
◆ Essay - Ian M. Ross

This Web site describes the development of the telephone and telecommunications industry in the twentieth century, covering topics such as long distance calling and cell phones.

Access this Web site from http://www.myreportlinks.com

In England, Sir Charles Wheatstone and Sir William Fothergill Cooke created a device that could send and receive messages over electrical wires. The electrical telegraph used needles that moved to represent messages. Wheatstone and Cooke's telegraph began operating on April 9, 1839, along a 13-mile (21-kilometer) section of the Great Western Railway.

In the United States, meanwhile, Samuel F. B. Morse was at work on his own version of an electrical telegraph. Morse's invention consisted of a transmitter and receiver of electrical pulses. The telegraph transmitter could send short electrical pulses, called dots, and long electrical pulses, called dashes, which were three times as long as the dots. Morse developed a code for sending messages on the telegraph. The Morse code consisted of variously spaced dots and dashes to represent the letters of the alphabet and numbers.

The telegraph operator tapped out a message in Morse code on the telegraph transmitter key. At the other end of the line, the telegraph receiver pressed the dots and dashes of the Morse code into a moving paper strip attached to the machine. Alfred Vail had invented this method of recording telegraph

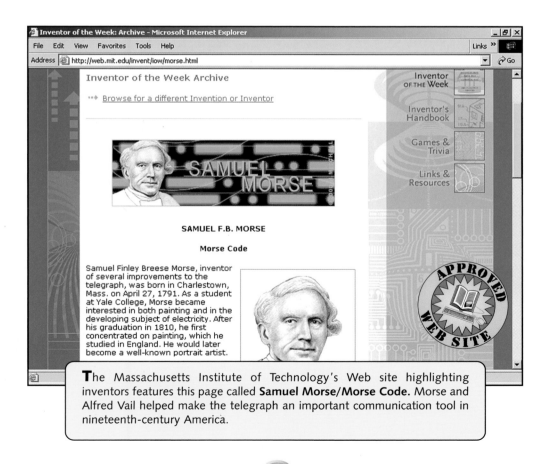

The Massachusetts Institute of Technology's Web site highlighting inventors features this page called **Samuel Morse/Morse Code.** Morse and Alfred Vail helped make the telegraph an important communication tool in nineteenth-century America.

messages, and Morse included it in his telegraph receiver.

⊜ MORSE IS GRANTED A PATENT

Morse first attempted to demonstrate his invention on September 2, 1837, in New York City. It was unsuccessful. But on January 6, 1838, he sent a telegraph message over a distance of three miles (five kilometers).

On June 20, 1840, Morse got a patent for the telegraph. (A patent is a legal document that gives

The **Telegraph Office** in Canso, Nova Scotia, around 1910. Despite the telephone's invention more than thirty years earlier, the telegraph was still an important way of delivering messages over a long distance.

an inventor the exclusive right to make, sell, and use an invention for a certain number of years.) Because of the patent, Morse is usually credited with inventing the telegraph. But as is often the case, an invention is rarely the work of just one person—inventors tend to make use of the ideas of other scientists and inventors.

Morse's telegraph built on the work of Wheatstone and Cooke as well as that of other scientists, including André Ampere of France, Alessandro Volta of Italy, and Joseph Henry of the United States. These men were pioneers in the field of electromagnetism who had experimented with sending electrical signals through wires. Morse combined and applied their discoveries in his own invention.

In 1842, the United States Congress agreed to spend thirty thousand dollars to build an experimental electric line between Washington, D.C., and Baltimore, Maryland, a distance of 40 miles (64 kilometers). On May 24, 1844, Morse demonstrated his telegraph over the new line. Using Morse code, he sent the message "What hath God wrought!"[1]

BREAKING THE BARRIERS OF DISTANCE

Morse's telegraph was a huge success. With western expansion, the country was growing rapidly in size and population. Morse's telegraph helped bring people from all parts of the country closer together. The new technology was vitally important to businessmen and politicians. Soon, telegraph companies were formed, and electric lines were strung at an amazing speed. By 1852, more than 20,000 miles (32,180 kilometers) of telegraph lines connected cities as far apart as Washington, D.C. and St. Louis. By 1861, more than 50,000 miles (80,460 kilometers) of wire stretched from the Atlantic Ocean to the Pacific Ocean.

People quickly came to depend on the telegraph. They called it the "wonder working wire."[2] Journalists could "wire," or send by telegraph, the home office of their newspaper with the latest

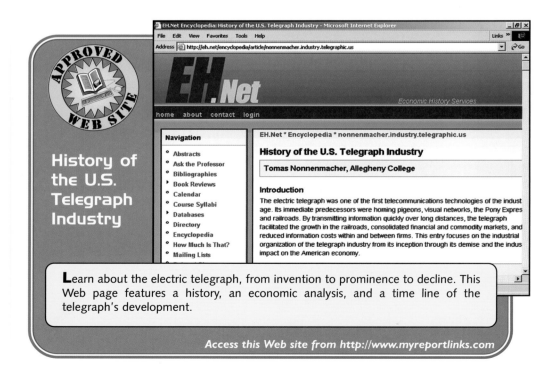

History of the U.S. Telegraph Industry

EH.Net Encyclopedia: History of the U.S. Telegraph Industry - Microsoft Internet Explorer

File   Edit   View   Favorites   Tools   Help   Links »

Address   http://eh.net/encyclopedia/article/nonnenmacher.industry.telegraphic.us   Go

EH.Net   Economic History Services

home   about   contact   login

Navigation

- Abstracts
- Ask the Professor
- Bibliographies
- Book Reviews
- Calendar
- Course Syllabi
- Databases
- Directory
- Encyclopedia
- How Much Is That?
- Mailing Lists

EH.Net * Encyclopedia * nonnenmacher.industry.telegraphic.us

History of the U.S. Telegraph Industry

Tomas Nonnenmacher, Allegheny College

Introduction

The electric telegraph was one of the first telecommunications technologies of the industrial age. Its immediate predecessors were homing pigeons, visual networks, the Pony Express and railroads. By transmitting information quickly over long distances, the telegraph facilitated the growth in the railroads, consolidated financial and commodity markets, and reduced information costs within and between firms. This entry focuses on the industrial organization of the telegraph industry from its inception through its demise and the industry impact on the American economy.

Learn about the electric telegraph, from invention to prominence to decline. This Web page features a history, an economic analysis, and a time line of the telegraph's development.

Access this Web site from http://www.myreportlinks.com

reports of breaking news. Businesspeople could send and receive orders and other information almost instantly. Investors from around the country could find out the latest stock prices from the New York Stock Exchange.

⊜ ON SCHEDULE

The ability to communicate quickly improved life in all sorts of ways. For example, the telegraph helped railroad managers create precise train schedules. Because most railroads had only a single set of tracks, accurate scheduling was necessary to prevent head-on collisions. Telegraph lines often ran along railroad tracks. Railroad managers could speed trains on their way when a track was clear and hold them when it was not. By 1860, almost every railroad station had a telegraph.

Quick communication became even more important during the American Civil War. In 1861, when the war began, President Abraham Lincoln sent a telegraph message calling for 75,000 troops to defend Washington, D.C. Lincoln received an immediate response informing him that 90,000 troops were ready. The military began using the telegraph to direct troop movements, provide logistical support and, in general, increase the efficiency and organization of operations. Military commanders also sent and received strategic and tactical intelligence about enemy troop movements. Communication had come a long way since the War of 1812.

→ THE TELEGRAPH MADE THE WORLD SMALLER

During the 1850s, efforts were made to link the United States and Europe by telegraph. This required laying 2,500 miles (4,023 kilometers) of cable under the Atlantic Ocean, a difficult and dangerous task. The first attempt in 1857, led by American businessman Cyrus Field, failed when the submarine cables snapped only 300 miles (482 kilometers) off the coast of Ireland. The next attempt in 1858 was successful—sort of. Britain's

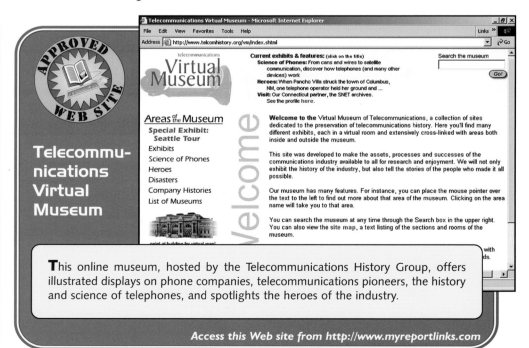

This online museum, hosted by the Telecommunications History Group, offers illustrated displays on phone companies, telecommunications pioneers, the history and science of telephones, and spotlights the heroes of the industry.

Access this Web site from http://www.myreportlinks.com

Queen Victoria, did send a message to President James Buchanan, which helped make the new technology more famous. And while more than seven hundred messages did pass between the United States and England, the cable snapped after just a few weeks.

⇒ Under the Sea

Before Field could organize an attempt to reconnect the underwater cable, the American Civil War began. Throughout the war, from 1861 to 1865, there was not enough money to repair or continue work on the transatlantic cable link because money was needed for the war effort.

But in 1866, a group of businessmen headed by Field raised money to build the world's largest ship. The steamship, called the Great Eastern, was big enough to hold the 2,000 miles (3,218 kilometers) of telegraph cable needed to connect Ireland and Newfoundland, Canada. The work began immediately and the cable was successfully completed on July 27, 1866.

By the 1880s, underwater cables linked the Americas, Europe, Africa, and Asia. The American federal government used the telegraph to monitor political and economic developments all over the world. The telegraph made it possible for the government to respond quickly whenever a serious crisis arose.

Quick communication between the United States and other countries around the world was a reality. American families in all parts of the country could send and receive messages to and from relatives scattered across the huge continent.

⊖ THE TELEGRAPH'S SHORTCOMINGS

As beneficial as the telegraph was, it had certain drawbacks that prevented it from becoming the medium of mass communication. First of all, the average person could not use it. Telegraph lines did not connect private homes.

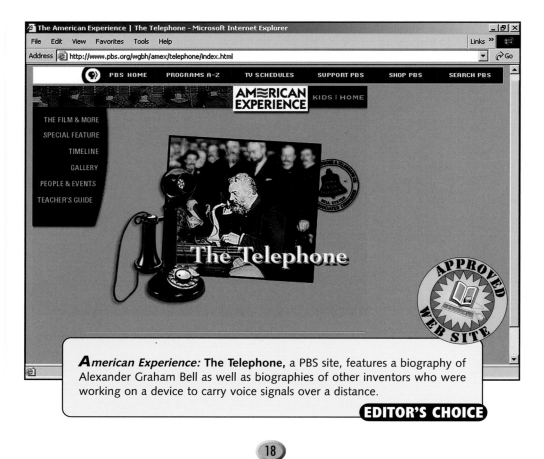

American Experience: The Telephone, a PBS site, features a biography of Alexander Graham Bell as well as biographies of other inventors who were working on a device to carry voice signals over a distance.

EDITOR'S CHOICE

It was also expensive: A one-page telegram could cost hundreds of dollars to send, so most people still wrote letters to communicate with people far away. And even if telegraphy, the system of using a telegraph to communicate, had not been so expensive, most people did not know Morse code, which itself limited the speed of telegraphic communication. It could take a minute to transmit a single sentence using Morse code. A news article could tie up the system for hours.

The telegraph was certainly a major advance in communication. But it did not bring about major changes to people's daily lives the way the telephone would. Alexander Graham Bell's machine truly conquered time and distance and helped create a world in which people were as close to each other as the nearest phone, no matter where on earth they were.

ALEXANDER GRAHAM BELL: THE EARLY YEARS

Alexander Graham Bell was born on March 3, 1847, in Edinburgh, Scotland. The man who would one day invent the telephone —and truly change the world— was born in an age where slow communication was normal and accepted. In 1847, the telegraph still had not reached Edinburgh.

CHAPTER

2

THE BELL FAMILY: THREE ALEXANDERS, TWO MELVILLES, BUT ONLY ONE GRAHAM

Giving many people the same name seems to have been a tradition in the Bell family. Alexander Graham Bell was named after his grandfather Alexander Bell. His father was named Alexander Melville Bell. His older brother, born in 1845, was named Melville. And his younger brother, born in 1848, was named Edward. The Alexander Bell who would invent the phone did not receive his middle name until later.

At the age of ten, young Alexander Bell met a family friend from Canada whose name was Alexander Graham. He was a former student of Alexander's father. Alexander Bell admired this man so much and liked his name that on March 3, 1858, Alexander's eleventh birthday, his father gave him the middle name Graham. Until this time, people had called him Aleck. From then on, some called him Graham although others, including his family, still called him Aleck.

→ A Fascination With Sounds

As an adult, Alexander Graham Bell recalled his earliest childhood memory: a family outing when he was four years old to a wheat field outside Edinburgh. Young Aleck had wandered off through the wheat, which was taller than he was. The soft sounds of the wheat swishing in the wind intrigued him. When Aleck had gone some distance from his family, he sat down and listened for any sounds in the quietness around him. Eventually, he got up and tried to find his way back to his family. But he could not see above the wheat and did not know which way to go. Lost, he lay down and cried himself to sleep.

"I was awakened by my father's voice," Bell recalled. " 'Aleck, Aleck,' he shouted in stentorian [loud] tones that effectually dispelled my slumbers."[1]

As a young boy, Aleck was interested in just about everything. He loved to spend time in the fields, woods, and hills near his home. He was curious about the wonders of nature. He wanted to know how birds could fly and how plants grew. He wondered what caused the waves in the ocean. Aleck and his older brother Melville collected plants and small dead animals, such as mice and toads, which they dissected to learn about their bodies.

But most of all, Aleck was fascinated by sound—all kinds of sounds, especially the sounds

▼ Bell grew up in Edinburgh, Scotland, in the mid-nineteenth century, curious about everything around him. Here, he is pictured (second from left) with his brothers, Melville and Edward, and his parents.

▲ *Alexander Bell, Aleck's grandfather, was a teacher of elocution, or the art of public speaking. He played a pivotal role in young Aleck's life.*

of speech and the sounds of music. It was not surprising that Aleck would have such an interest. After all, both his father and grandfather were teachers of elocution—the art of public speaking.

Aleck's grandfather helped people to overcome speech defects such as stammering and lisps. Aleck's father taught speech at the University of Edinburgh. He wrote many books on speech and was considered an expert in the field. His book *The*

Standard Elocutionist, written in 1860, sold more than 750,000 copies. Aleck's mother, Eliza Grace, was nearly deaf, and his father was especially interested in helping the deaf to speak. He had invented a system called Visible Speech.

Because Eliza was hard of hearing, she used a rubber ear tube, a hearing device that she held up to her ear. When a person spoke into the large end, the hearing tube funneled the sound toward Eliza's eardrum. As Aleck grew and his voice changed, he discovered that Eliza could understand what he was saying if he spoke in low, steady tones right against her forehead. Apparently, she was able to detect the vibrations of his speech.

How We Hear— And Why Some of Us Cannot

To understand Alexander Graham Bell's fascination with sound, which ultimately led to his invention of the telephone, it is important to understand how the human ear works.

Our ears have three main parts: the outer ear, which is visible, the middle ear, and the inner ear. The main job of the outer ear, called the auricle or pinna, is to collect sounds. The outer ear opens into the ear canal, a tubed passageway. After sound waves enter the outer ear, they travel through the ear canal and make their way to the middle ear and the eardrum, a piece of skin or

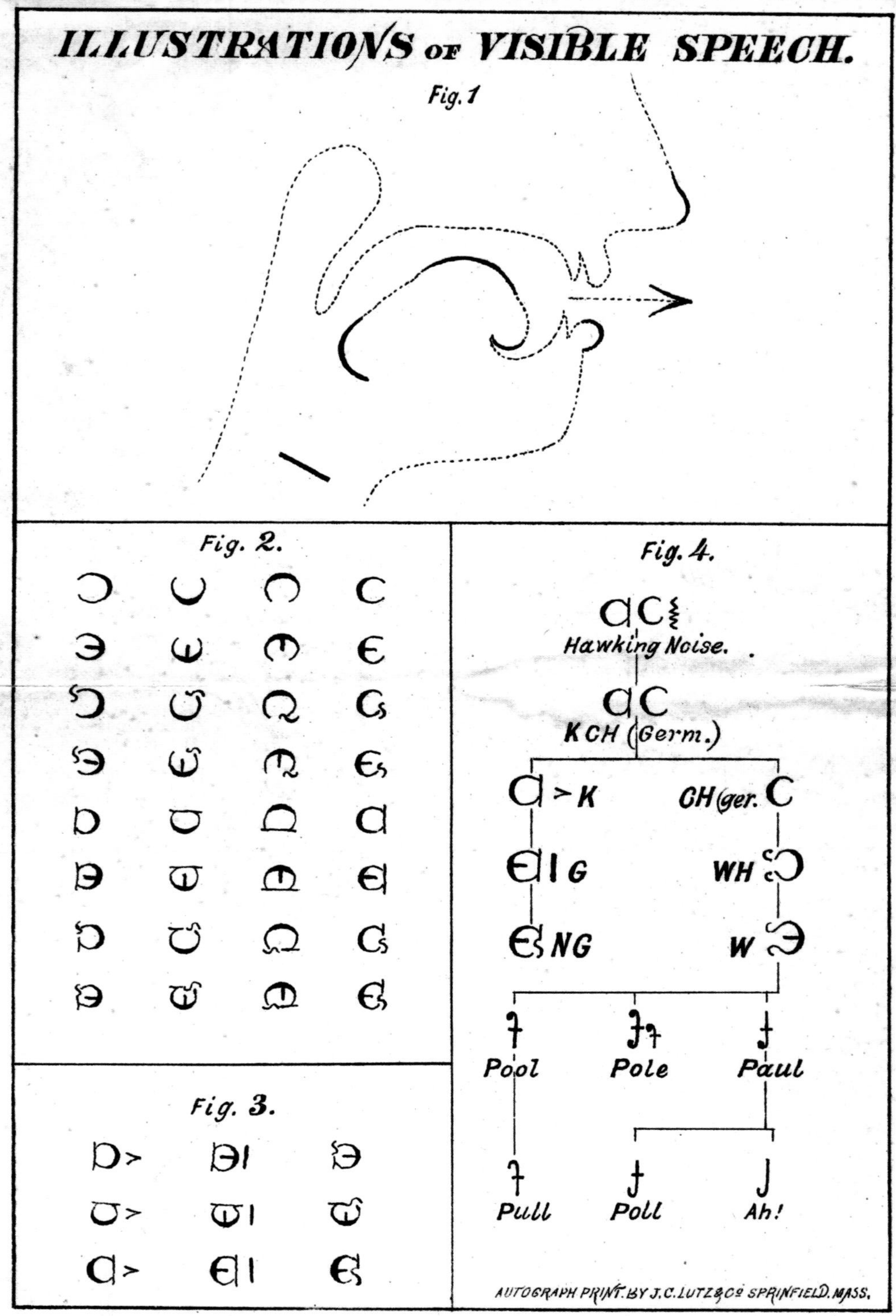

ILLUSTRATIONS of VISIBLE SPEECH.

Fig. 1

Fig. 2.

Fig. 4.

Hawking Noise.

K CH (Germ.)

> K — CH (ger.)

I G — WH

NG — W

Pool — Pole — Paul

Pull — Poll — Ah!

AUTOGRAPH PRINT BY J.C. LUTZ & Cº SPRINFIELD. MASS.

Fig. 3.

It was no surprise that Bell was fascinated with sound. Eliza Grace Bell, Aleck's mother, was nearly deaf. Her husband, Melville Bell, devised a system known as Visible Speech to help people like her translate images into sounds.

membrane that is stretched tight. The eardrum separates the outer ear from the middle ear and three tiny bones known as ossicles. These bones are the three smallest bones in your body.

When sound waves reach the eardrum, it vibrates, moving these tiny bones, which in turn move the vibrations along on their journey to the inner ear. It is the inner ear that contains the auditory, or hearing nerve, which connects to our brains. The auditory nerve transforms the vibrations into nerve impulses. These impulses travel directly to our brain, which interprets them as sound.

There are different reasons why people cannot hear. They may be born deaf, or they may lose their hearing because of injury or disease. They may also suffer injury to that part of their brain which would normally translate messages from the nerves in the ear into sound. Sound—a fascination with it, a curiosity about it, and a desire to transform it for those unable to hear it—would play a large role in the life of Alexander Graham Bell.

➔A Love for Music

Throughout his childhood, Aleck was a dreamer. His father wanted him to take his studies more seriously, but school bored Aleck, who preferred to learn about the world directly from his observations of nature rather than from textbooks. One of his favorite spots was Corstorphine Hill, just a couple of miles from his home. Years later, Aleck wrote, "In boyhood, I . . . spent many happy hours lying among the heather on the Scottish hills—breathing in the scenery around me with a quiet delight that is even now pleasant for me to remember."[2] While Aleck's father frowned on his son's wanderings, his mother Eliza supported them.

⇒ PIANO MAN

Eliza was an accomplished artist, and despite being hard of hearing, she was an excellent pianist. She encouraged a love of music in her three sons. But only Aleck had a gift for playing the piano. He could play by ear and improvise. Eliza gave Aleck his first piano lessons and he made rapid progress.

When Aleck turned ten, his mother arranged for him to take piano lessons with Auguste Benoit Bertini, a famous pianist. Bertini felt that Aleck showed enough promise to consider a professional career and Aleck Bell loved music so much that, at the time, his fondest dream was to become a concert pianist.

Aleck's father, however, did not approve. He saw nothing wrong with playing the piano as a hobby. But he believed that serious studies in the pursuit of an academic career would be a much

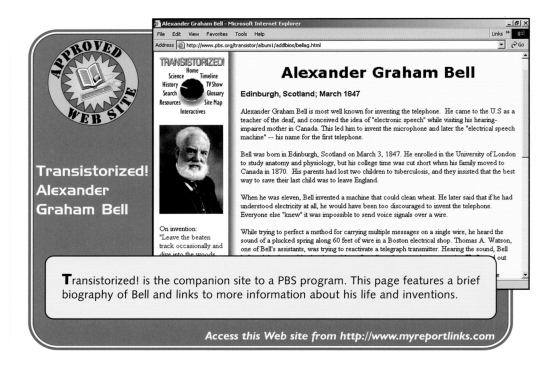

Transistorized!
Alexander
Graham Bell

Transistorized! is the companion site to a PBS program. This page features a brief biography of Bell and links to more information about his life and inventions.

Access this Web site from http://www.myreportlinks.com

more worthy goal. Aleck later told an interviewer, "My dream as a young man was to become a musician and I used to smile in a superior way at the plans of my family to make something else of me."[3]

But as it turned out, Bertini died before Aleck had gone very far down the path toward the concert hall. And he never took lessons from another teacher.

In 1858, Aleck entered Edinburgh's Royal High School. During his four years there, he had to study Latin and Greek, which he hated. He was bored with his math courses. And even the courses in chemistry and natural history held little interest for him. All in all, Aleck was not an outstanding student. As he would later write, "I passed through the whole curriculum of the Royal High School, from the lowest to the highest class, and graduated, but by no means with honors, when I was about fourteen years of age."[4]

⇒ ALECK'S FIRST INVENTION

Not far from the Bell family home in Edinburgh was a flour mill, owned by John Herdman, the father of one of Aleck's friends, Ben Herdman. Aleck and Ben often made a mess playing in the mill. One day, tired of cleaning up after them, John Herdman dragged the young boys into his office to scold them. Years later, Aleck reported that Herdman had demanded, "Now boys, why don't you do something useful?"[5] Herdman then said that he and his workmen had not been able to find a way to easily separate the husks from the grain, which is ground up to make flour. "If you could only take the husks off this wheat you would be of some help."[6]

Aleck and Ben found that they could scrape the husks off the grain with a small nailbrush, usually used to clean fingernails. They then devised a system for doing the job on a much larger scale. They found an old barrel with a rotating paddle wheel inside, to which they attached rough, short-bristled brushes. As they poured grain into the vat, they cranked a handle that rotated the paddles.

The process separated the wheat berries from the husks. Aleck was amazed that the invention worked! And Herdman was very happy. Years later, Aleck said, "Herdman's injunction [order] to 'do something useful' was my first incentive to invention, and the method of cleaning wheat the first fruits."[7]

A Year to Remember

In 1862, when Aleck was fifteen, Alexander Melville sent him to live with his grandfather

Alexander Bell in London for a year. Aleck's father hoped that the boy's grandfather would be a good influence on him. There is no doubt that Aleck's grandfather had a profound influence on the young man. Alexander Bell gave his grandson lessons in elocution, Shakespeare, and the treatment of speech defects. He insisted

Bell at age fourteen. While at Edinburgh's Royal High School, most subjects bored Aleck and he was just an average student.

that Aleck dress in formal clothes when walking around London and that he carry a cane.

When Alexander Melville came to bring Aleck home at the end of the year, he noticed a big change in his son. It seemed that Aleck had been transformed into a serious, studious young gentleman. Aleck himself later commented that the year with his grandfather "converted me from a boy somewhat prematurely into a man."[8]

➡ MACHINES THAT SPEAK

Before returning to Edinburgh, Alexander Melville took his son to visit Sir Charles Wheatstone, the famous scientist who had invented an early telegraph machine. Wheatstone had also built a mechanical speaking machine that could pronounce human words. Although the machine's speech was crude, it made a great impression on Aleck.

Back in Edinburgh, Alexander Melville challenged his sons to build their own speaking machine. He wanted them to build one that could produce clearer and more accurate speech than Wheatstone's machine. He believed that this project would help his sons understand how the sounds of a voice are produced.

Sixteen-year-old Aleck and eighteen-year-old Melville, nicknamed Melly, tackled the job together, dividing the work. Aleck made the

Grand papa's Birth Place.
ST ANDREWS.

Home, 10th October, 1862.

My Dear Aleck

Your leaving us today makes the first break in our family. I thank God, that this break is not attended by any circumstances, retrospective or prospective, which can cause us uneasiness or anxiety on your account. You go to reside for a time with my dear father, where I trust that you will feel — not so much that you have left home, as — that you have only gone, as it were, from one room of your home to another. We shall miss you, my dear boy. You have been a good son, — loving and obedient. If occasional clouds and showers have crossed the zenith in our united life, these have only refreshed our love, and fertilized your character to a richer growth. You leave none but happy

▲ Melville Bell wrote this letter in 1862 to his son after Aleck had gone to stay with his grandfather. Melville Bell noted that his son's leaving "makes the first break in our family," but hoped that his son would not be homesick, but rather feel that he had only gone from "one room of [his] home to another."

machine's tongue and mouth. Melly made the lungs and throat. The boys modeled their machine after a human skull. They used various materials for different parts of the machine. For example, the tongue and lips were made of rubber covering wood and wire and stuffed with cotton. They built a keyboard to control the parts.

➲ TEACH AN OLD DOG NEW TRICKS

When Aleck and Melly finished their machine, they placed it on the steps outside their house and made it speak. Aleck later wrote that:

> It really sounded like a baby in great distress. 'Mamma, Mamma' came forth with heart-rending effect. We heard someone above say, 'Good gracious, what can be the matter with that baby,' and then footsteps were heard. This, of course, was just what we wanted. We quietly slipped into our house, and closed the door, leaving our neighbors to pursue their fruitless quest for the baby. Our triumph and happiness were complete.[9]

Much later, Alexander Graham Bell wrote, "The making of this talking-machine certainly marked an important point in my career. It made me familiar with the functions of the vocal cords, and started me along the path that led to the telephone."[10]

After working very hard to complete the talking machine, Aleck and Melly decided to have some fun by trying to teach their family dog to "talk." First

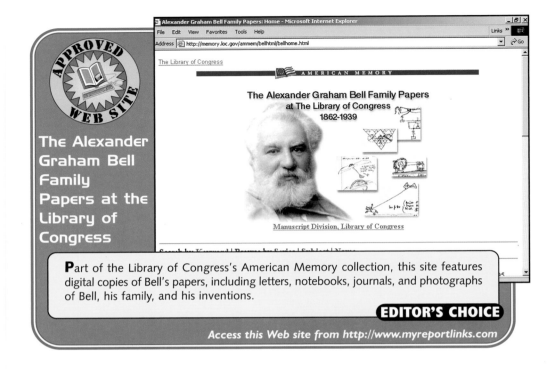

The Library of Congress

AMERICAN MEMORY

The Alexander Graham Bell Family Papers
at The Library of Congress
1862-1939

Manuscript Division, Library of Congress

The Alexander Graham Bell Family Papers at the Library of Congress

Part of the Library of Congress's American Memory collection, this site features digital copies of Bell's papers, including letters, notebooks, journals, and photographs of Bell, his family, and his inventions.

EDITOR'S CHOICE

Access this Web site from http://www.myreportlinks.com

they taught the dog to growl on command. Then Aleck took the dog's mouth in his hands, opening and closing its lips while he was growling. The dog now seemed to say "ma ma ma ma," sounding very much like a young child's crying. The boys kept experimenting with the dog, manipulating his jaw, holding his lips, and massaging and poking his vocal chords. They got the dog to form various vowel and consonant sounds, such as "ow," "ah," "ga," "gr," and "oo." Eventually, the dog was able to say "How are you, grand-mamma?" which was pronounced "ow ah oo, ga-ma-ma."[11]

Some of Aleck's family were impressed with the "talking" dog. They thought the dog even sounded better than the talking machine the boys had built. But Aleck's father was not amused. He thought his sons were making fun of his Visible Speech system.

⇒ VISIBLE SPEECH

For the past fifteen years, Alexander Melville Bell had been working on a system that would teach people who could not hear and speak how to communicate. He had created an alphabet of thirty-four symbols to represent the sounds the human voice made. The symbols were a visual representation of sound. They showed how the palate, tongue, and teeth are positioned when saying a particular word. A deaf person who learned Bell's Visible Speech could articulate the words that were spelled out beneath the symbols. Visible Speech could be used to represent any language and could also teach deaf people how to understand what other people said by the motions of their lips.

Alexander Melville Bell taught Visible Speech to Aleck and Melly. When he went on tour to demonstrate the system, his sons accompanied him and assisted him in the demonstrations. Meanwhile, Aleck became very involved with schoolwork—both as a student and as a teacher. In 1863, he

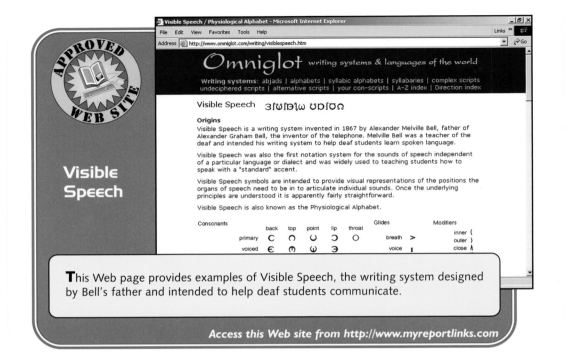

This Web page provides examples of Visible Speech, the writing system designed by Bell's father and intended to help deaf students communicate.

Access this Web site from http://www.myreportlinks.com

began teaching speech and music at Weston House Academy in Elgin, Scotland. Some of sixteen-year-old Aleck's students were older than he was, but they did not know it. Between his two years at Elgin, Aleck studied at the University of Edinburgh. He took classes in Greek, Latin, and physics, subjects he had once hated. He also studied anatomy, with a focus on the ear, mouth, nose, and throat.

During Aleck's second year at Elgin, he conducted experiments using tuning forks to learn more about how sounds are produced. He discovered that when a tuning fork is struck, it vibrates and produces a tone. When one tuning fork vibrates, another tuning fork with the same tone will vibrate. Aleck learned that the German scientist Hermann von Helmholtz had also conducted experiments with tuning forks. When Aleck read Helmholtz's paper describing his experiments, he made a mistake in the translation from German. Somehow, Aleck got the idea that Helmholtz had transmitted vowel sounds electrically over telegraph wires. He came to believe that someday speech would be sent over a telegraph wire. And he hoped to be the person to invent a "talking telegraph."

⇒ GOOD VIBRATIONS

Aleck also wanted to learn whether or not vowel sounds are made up of more than one tone. He made instruments with stretched membranes to measure the vibrations in the air produced by human speech. He discovered that vowel sounds are compound. Years later he recalled, "These experiments paved the way for the appearance of the first membrane telephone, the ancestor of all the telephones of today."[12]

In 1866, Bell took a teaching job in Bath, England. His grandfather had died the previous year, and Bell's family moved from Edinburgh to London. In 1867, the Bell family suffered another loss: Edward died of tuberculosis, a highly contagious disease that affects the lungs. Though saddened by his younger brother's death, Bell kept working hard. In 1868, he went to work at the London School for the Deaf. There he used his father's Visible Speech system to teach deaf children. He was so successful that parents of deaf children flocked to the school, eager to enroll their kids.

But Alexander Graham Bell's success was soon tempered by yet another family tragedy: In 1870, his brother Melly became ill with tuberculosis and died soon after. Bell's parents believed the smoggy, damp air of London was partly to blame for their sons' deaths. When Bell began to show the same symptoms, growing weak and coughing frequently, his parents became alarmed.

▽ *Edinburgh, Scotland, in the late nineteenth century. Bell studied at the University of Edinburgh between teaching speech and music at an academy in Elgin, about 175 miles north of the Scottish capital.*

Bell was devastated by the loss of his brothers. ▷
His family's decision to move from England to
Canada soon after dealt the young Bell
another difficult blow.

Alexander Melville Bell had recently taken a trip to Canada and the United States. He had been impressed by these quickly growing countries. Hoping that the climate there would improve his son's health, Alexander Melville Bell decided to move his family. In July of 1870, the Bell family set sail for Canada.

Bell was sad to leave behind everything that meant anything to him—his work and his students in particular. He grieved so deeply over the loss of his brothers that for the moment, he even seemed to lose interest in his experiments and ideas for inventions. Nor did he believe the New World would have anything worthwhile to offer.

Experiments With Telegraphy

In August 1870, the Bell family settled in Brantford, Ontario, 45 miles (72 kilometers) west of Buffalo, New York. At first, Bell struggled to find the will to go on with his life. "I went to Canada to die,"[1] he said, referring to his feelings at the time. He was sick in both body and spirit, and he sorely missed his brother Melly. He was also homesick: His strange surroundings made Bell realize how much he missed England and Scotland. He wondered if he would ever have the strength to work again.

Teaching the Deaf to Speak

Bell's father went on a tour of several cities in Canada and the United States, giving lectures and demonstrations of Visible Speech. In Boston, he was offered a job at the Boston School for Deaf-Mutes. Not interested in the job, the elder Bell recommended his son for the position and signed him up. The job, a temporary position, involved teaching Visible Speech to the faculty at the school.

CHAPTER

3

In April 1871, Alexander Graham Bell moved to Boston to work at the Boston School for Deaf-Mutes. After spending a month training teachers, Bell took a permanent job at the school. Although he now worked with both adults and children who were deaf, he seemed to have more success with the children. Bell was highly motivated to help the children. He learned sign language, which he found useful in speaking to groups of deaf-mutes. At the time, he wrote his family, "It makes my very heart ache to see the

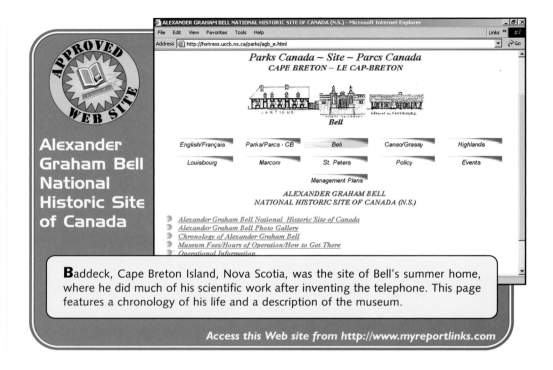

Alexander Graham Bell National Historic Site of Canada

Baddeck, Cape Breton Island, Nova Scotia, was the site of Bell's summer home, where he did much of his scientific work after inventing the telephone. This page features a chronology of his life and a description of the museum.

Access this Web site from http://www.myreportlinks.com

difficulties the little children have to contend with on account of the prejudice of their teachers. You know that here all communication is strictly with the mouth . . . and just fancy little children who have no idea of speech being made dependent on lip-reading for almost every idea that enters their heads."[2]

In the fall of 1872, Bell quit his regular teaching job and took on private students instead. He believed that this would enable him to earn more money. Bell's first private student was a five-year-old boy named George Sanders. The boy was the son of Thomas Sanders, a wealthy leather goods merchant from Salem, Massachusetts. George Sanders had been born totally deaf and had never spoken a word in his life. To be close to Bell, the boy and his nurse moved into a house next door.

Bell used a two-track approach to teach George to speak. He created a series of flash cards with pictures and words of familiar things, such as "man" and "shoe." At the same time, he devised a special glove for George that had the twenty-six letters of the alphabet printed on it. Using the glove, Bell taught George the letters of the alphabet. The two learned to communicate with each

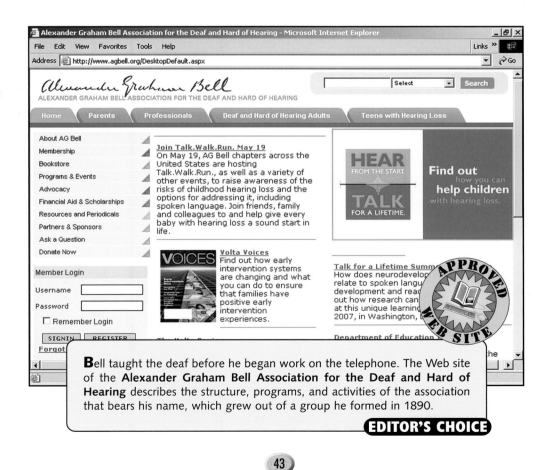

Bell taught the deaf before he began work on the telephone. The Web site of the **Alexander Graham Bell Association for the Deaf and Hard of Hearing** describes the structure, programs, and activities of the association that bears his name, which grew out of a group he formed in 1890.

EDITOR'S CHOICE

other by pointing to the letters on the glove to form words. Bell's strategy proved to be a great success. Thomas Sanders was thrilled with the progress his son made.

THE HARMONIC TELEGRAPH

Bell found Boston exciting. And with its fine universities and libraries, he considered it the intellectual center of the United States. He attended lectures at the Massachusetts Institute of Technology in Cambridge, where he had access to a laboratory and equipment that he could use to conduct experiments. It is no wonder that even while he was busy teaching George Sanders, new

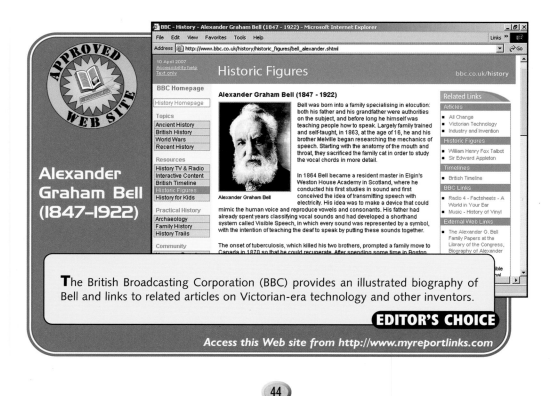

Alexander
Graham Bell
(1847–1922)

The British Broadcasting Corporation (BBC) provides an illustrated biography of Bell and links to related articles on Victorian-era technology and other inventors.

EDITOR'S CHOICE

Access this Web site from http://www.myreportlinks.com

ideas for inventions and experiments snuck into his head. Before long, Bell began experimenting with telegraphy.

In 1872, Bell was well aware of current developments in telegraphy. He knew about the duplex telegraph that had been invented by Joseph B. Stearns in 1867 and which could send two messages over the same wire at the same time. In 1872, Stearns sold the duplex telegraph to the Western Union Telegraph Company. Bell also knew that Western Union was supporting the experiments of Elisha Gray, who had invented an improved telegraph relay, or switch, in 1867. Bell decided to focus on inventing an improved telegraph that could send more than two messages over a single wire at the same time.

⇒ Name That Tune

Bell began working with tuning forks, circuits, and batteries. He believed that two different tones, produced by two vibrating tuning forks, could be transmitted simultaneously over the same electric wire. Those signals would then cause tuning forks at the receiving end to vibrate. Bell reasoned that using the same principle, he should be able to send hundreds of signals down a single wire by using hundreds of tuning forks.

Bell hoped to send Morse code messages by interrupting the vibrations of the tuning forks with dots and dashes. The tuning forks at the other end should click on and off, reproducing the same patterns of dashes and dots. Bell called this idea of a multiple telegraph the "harmonic" telegraph because the tones of the transmitted signals would be created by the harmonic tones of the tuning forks.

Bell continued working on the harmonic telegraph. But, as he did, he became even more interested in another idea—the "talking" telegraph, or the transmission of a human voice over a wire. Meanwhile, Bell kept busy teaching George Sanders and other private students during the day, while working on his inventions at night. He also taught students at the Clarke School for the Deaf in Northampton, Massachusetts. In 1873, he was appointed Professor of Vocal Physiology at Boston University, and he also gave lectures at MIT.

➲Important Relationships Begin

In 1873, the president of the Clarke School for the Deaf, Gardiner Greene Hubbard, asked Bell to teach his sixteen-year-old daughter, Mabel. She had become totally deaf at age five as a result of scarlet fever. Although she could lip-read, her speech was slurred. Bell agreed to work with Mabel, who would become a very important person in his life.

In 1874, Bell applied for a patent for his harmonic telegraph, but the request was rejected. His

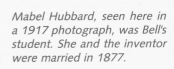

Mabel Hubbard, seen here in a 1917 photograph, was Bell's student. She and the inventor were married in 1877.

Birth of the Society @ nationalgeographic.com - Microsoft Internet Explorer

File   Edit   View   Favorites   Tools   Help

Address http://www.nationalgeographic.com/birth/nfor5at1.html   Go

Gardiner **Greene Hubbard** was the president of a school for the deaf and later the first president of the National Geographic Society. This picture of Hubbard, whose daughter, Mabel, was one of Bell's students, is featured on the *National Geographic* Web site.

idea for a telegraph that could transmit hundreds of messages was interesting, but he had not yet built a working model. Bell had encountered technical problems he had not been able to solve. He became discouraged and frustrated with his lack of progress.

Then one day, Bell met someone who would play an extremely important role in his career. While working on his harmonic telegraph, Bell had bought electrical equipment from the Charles Williams Electrical Supply Company, where he met Thomas Watson, a young electrical engineer who worked in Williams's shop. When Bell described what he was working on, Watson grew interested. The two had long discussions. Bell was impressed by Watson's mechanical ability and knowledge of electricity. The young engineer possessed an expertise in electricity that Bell lacked. Watson, on the other hand, was impressed with Bell's knowledge of sound. Bell hired Watson as his part-time assistant, and the two began working together on Bell's harmonic telegraph.

⇨ An Improved "Sound Writer"

During the summer of 1874, Bell took a vacation at his parents' home in Brantford, Ontario. In the course of working on his harmonic telegraph, he had studied a machine known as the phonautograph, literally a "sound writer," which was the earliest kind of phonographic recording device. It consisted of a hollow cylinder with a membrane stretched over one end. A stylus, or needle, was attached at the same end. When words were spoken into a tube at the other end of the cylinder, the membrane vibrated. This caused the stylus to move, inscribing lines on a smoked glass plate. The lines corresponded to the spoken words, creating a visual image that conveyed their meaning. Bell believed such a device could be used to help deaf people learn to speak. They

A 1902 photograph of Thomas Watson, Bell's assistant. Like Bell, Watson had no desire to become involved with the telecommunications industry after the invention of the telephone. He went on to head the largest shipyard in America, but an interest in acting led him to form his own troupe and write plays.

could compare the tracings of their own vocal sounds with tracings of standard pronunciations of words.

At his parents' home, Bell built his own improved version of a phonautograph. He wondered if a membrane receiver could be modeled after the human ear. After all, the human ear seemed to be the perfect instrument for detecting and recording sound. So for the membrane, Bell used an actual human ear from a corpse, given to him by Dr. Clarence J. Blake, a surgeon who conducted research in audiology, the branch of science that deals with hearing.

In what must have been a strange sight, Bell connected a piece of straw to the delicate bones of the corpse's inner ear, and then shouted, spoke, whispered, and sang into it. As sound waves moved the bones, the other end of the straw traced waveforms, shapes representing the characteristics of waves, on the plate. Bell was impressed by the ability of sound to move the stylus. As bizarre as this human-ear phonautograph was, it marked an important step on the road toward Bell's invention of the telephone.

⇒ A Partnership

In the fall of 1874, Thomas Sanders, who had become a great admirer of Bell, proposed a business partnership with the young inventor. He promised

Now the thought struck me
that if we could make the
direct and reversed induced
impulses succeed one another
as regularly as the crests
and depressions of waves
— then an electrode applied
to the ear so as to induce
a vibration in the membrane
tymp. — should create the
sensation of sound without
the aid of any intermediate
apparatus.

I have had an instrument
made and the experiment
seems a success.

A number of permanent
magnets were arranged

to finance Bell in return for a share in the patent rights to his inventions. Around the same time, Gardiner Hubbard, Mabel's father, also proposed a partnership. Hubbard was a lawyer with expertise in patents. He had long been interested in tele- graphy and believed Bell's work showed a lot of promise. On February 27, 1875, an agreement

◀ *In this letter to Dr. Clarence Blake, (left, and below), Bell described his idea for an improved phonautograph, the earliest kind of phonographic recording device, and included a basic sketch.*

upon a cylinder (see illustration)

(I hope you admire my drawing!!!)

which was revolved in front of electro-magnets. On filling my ears with water and applying the wires (protected) as in the diagram, a soft musical note was heard. The sound stopped the moment the electrical current was broken. The wires employed were very short, so that the noise of the among the three men was drawn up and signed. The partnership became known as the Bell Patent Association.

Once he had financing, Bell decided to devote most of his time to inventing. He dropped most of his students, except for George Sanders, Mabel Hubbard, and a few others, and he stopped lecturing. Sanders and Hubbard believed that Bell's best chance for success lay in the completion of his work on the harmonic telegraph. At the time, other inventors including Thomas Edison and Elisha Gray were racing to patent their own versions of a multiple telegraph.

In 1874, Gray had invented an electromagnetic device for transmitting musical tones. Gray claimed to have sent eight tones over the same wire, a process described by the *New York Times* as "music by telegraph." Gray demonstrated the device at the Presbyterian Church in Highland Park, Illinois, where he gave a lecture about the possibility of transmitting speech.

⊜ PERFECT HARMONY

Sanders and Hubbard both wanted Bell to continue working on the harmonic telegraph and he agreed to keep working on that project. But even as he and Watson tried to perfect the harmonic telegraph, Bell was becoming more and more interested in the talking telegraph. A device that

INVENTING THE TELEPHONE

Bell had gained valuable insights into the nature of speech and sound while working on the phonautograph. He learned that speech, a complex series of unbroken waves in the air, could not be transmitted by conventional telegraphs. It also occurred to Bell that sound itself might be powerful enough to control an electric current.

Bell wondered if the human voice was powerful enough to create strong electrical impulses all by itself. If so, would this make the talking telegraph possible? The trick would be to change the sound waves into electrical current in the transmitter, sending the varying electric signal to the other end of a telegraph line and converting it back to sound waves. Bell knew that the human

CHAPTER

4

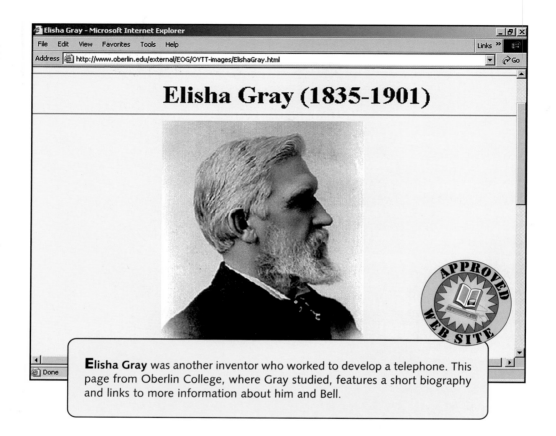

Elisha Gray - Microsoft Internet Explorer

File   Edit   View   Favorites   Tools   Help   Links »

Address http://www.oberlin.edu/external/EOG/OYTT-images/ElishaGray.html   Go

Elisha Gray (1835-1901)

Elisha Gray was another inventor who worked to develop a telephone. This page from Oberlin College, where Gray studied, features a short biography and links to more information about him and Bell.

could reproduce and transmit human speech and sound waves seemed much more important to him than a harmonic telegraph. The talking telegraph would soon become the main focus of Bell's inventive genius.

ear converts sound waves into electrical pulses, letting us hear. So his transmitter would have to do the same thing. If somehow Bell were able to accomplish all of this, he would have his talking telegraph. But the question was, how? While pondering the possibility of building a working model of the talking telegraph, Bell decided he would call his invention the "telephone."

→ TELEPHONES OF OTHER INVENTORS

Bell did not invent the word "telephone," nor did he invent the idea of one. The Greek roots of the word telephone mean "far-speaking," so telephone is a perfect word to describe vocal communication over a distance. Long before Bell became interested in the telegraph and the telephone, others were busy inventing their own versions of the telephone. None

One of the most famous photographs of Alexander Graham Bell, taken in 1904.

of them, however, succeeded in creating a device that would be practical.

In 1849, Antonio Meucci, an Italian inventor living in Havana, Cuba, demonstrated a device that he later called a telephone. Meucci's invention involved the electrical transmission of voice over a copper wire. Meucci had been experimenting with methods of treating illness with electric shocks when he discovered that sounds could travel through copper wire. But Meucci's telephone was impractical, requiring direct electrical connections to people. The user had to place the receiver in his or her mouth to "hear" what was being said.

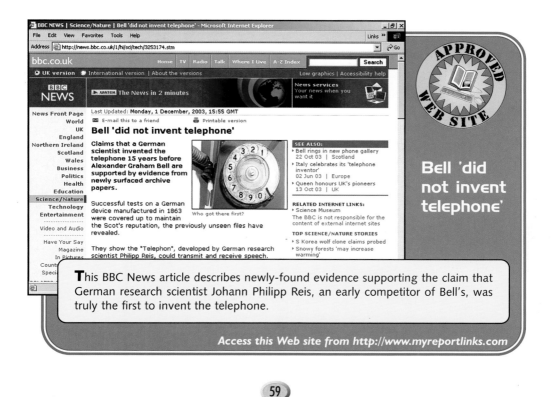

This BBC News article describes newly-found evidence supporting the claim that German research scientist Johann Philipp Reis, an early competitor of Bell's, was truly the first to invent the telephone.

Access this Web site from http://www.myreportlinks.com

In the 1850s, Meucci continued his work in Staten Island, New York. In 1855, he devised a telephone system running between his workshop and several rooms in his house next door so that he could communicate with his wife, who was partially paralyzed. Five years later, he demonstrated his telephone in New York. Listeners were able to hear the voice of a singer some distance away.

In 1871, Meucci filed for a caveat, a notice of intent to apply for a patent. However, he did not have the money for a patent, which cost $250, a lot of money in those days. Once he secured the caveat, Meucci attempted to interest the Western Union Telegraph Company in his invention. He hoped they would test his "talking telegraph" over their telegraph lines. Unfortunately for Meucci, Western Union was not interested.

⇒VIVE LA FRANCE

In 1854, Charles Bourseul, a Frenchman, had proposed the development of an electric telephone. He wrote, "I have . . . asked myself whether speech itself may be transmitted by electricity—in a word, if what is spoken in Vienna may not be heard in Paris. . . . Suppose that a man speaks near a movable disk, sufficiently flexible to lose none of the vibrations of the voice, that this disk alternately makes and breaks the currents from a battery: you may have at a distance another disk, which will simultaneously execute the same vibrations."[1] Bourseul's ideas were exciting, but he never conducted experiments to learn whether or not his theory would work.

In 1861, Johann Philipp Reis, a German inventor, developed a device that could transmit tones down an electric wire. Reis wrote, "I succeeded in inventing an apparatus, by which it is possible to make clear and evident the organs of hearing, but with which also one can reproduce tones of all kinds at any desired distance by means of the galvanic current. I named the instrument 'Telephon.' "[2]

Reis's telephone was not capable of transmitting human speech. Its "make-or-break" circuit worked only for simple sounds and short musical tones. If Reis had had a better understanding of how sound is transmitted by electricity, his invention could have been made to transmit speech. Had he tightened the electrical contacts on the diaphragm, a thin flexible disk that vibrates when struck with sound waves, he would have created the constant, unbroken current necessary for the transmission of speech.

➲ The Great Race

On November 23, 1874, Bell wrote a letter to his parents describing the race to develop the multiple or harmonic telegraph.

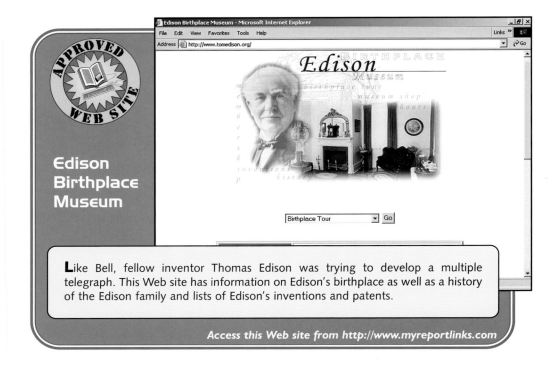

Like Bell, fellow inventor Thomas Edison was trying to develop a multiple telegraph. This Web site has information on Edison's birthplace as well as a history of the Edison family and lists of Edison's inventions and patents.

Access this Web site from http://www.myreportlinks.com

It is a neck and neck race between Mr. Gray and myself who shall complete our apparatus first. He has the advantage over me in being a practical electrician—but I have reason to believe that I am better acquainted with the phenomena of sound than he is—so that I have an advantage there. . . . The very opposition seems to nerve me to work and I feel with the facilities I have now I may succeed. Portions of my apparatus will be ready for trial tomorrow. However we shall see. I feel I shall be seriously ill should I fail in this now I am so thoroughly wrought up.[3]

In that same letter, Bell also described his idea for a talking telegraph or telephone. He wrote, "The idea to which I allude is an instrument by which the human voice might be telegraphed without the use of a battery at all. . . . The vibrations of a permanent magnet will induce a vibrating current of electricity in the coils of an electromagnet."[4]

In 1875, Bell and Watson attempted to build a working model of the harmonic telegraph (Watson now worked full-time for Bell). They had rented the small attic above Charles Williams's shop to conduct their experiments. They also planned to develop a talking telegraph. But Watson felt that tones would be easier to transmit than a human voice, so the two concentrated on the harmonic telegraph.

Bell and Watson knew that Elisha Gray was working on a multiple telegraph and both Gray and Thomas Edison were also working individually on a talking telegraph. So Bell and Watson were very well aware that they were in the race of their lives. The stakes were high: Whoever succeeded in building and patenting the first multiple telegraph would most likely gain fame and fortune beyond their wildest dreams.

⇒ TRIAL AND ERROR

But no matter how hard they tried, Bell and Watson had not been able to perfect their device. As the months of intensive labor passed, their frustration mounted. It seemed as if the multiple messages sent simultaneously over the same wire always got jumbled together. The resulting transmission was always garbled at the receiving end. Bell and Watson were beginning to think that a working harmonic telegraph was impossible.

One day when they had become especially discouraged, Bell stopped tinkering with the device. As Watson later wrote in his autobiography, Bell said, "Watson, I want to tell you of another idea which I think will surprise you. . . . If I could make a current of electricity vary in intensity, precisely as air varies in density during the production of a sound, I would be able to transmit speech electrically."[5]

So far, the two inventors had only succeeded in sending two simultaneous messages down the same wire in the form of on-and-off clicks of Morse code. They were still working to perfect the transmission of three simultaneous messages—a far cry from Bell's original goal of sending hundreds of simultaneous messages. Bell tried to interest Western Union in his device, but the company's managers were not. The company was putting all of its considerable support behind the efforts of Elisha Gray.

An Accidental Discovery

On June 2, 1875, it was unbearably hot and stuffy in the small attic above Charles Williams's shop. Bell and Watson could hardly breathe. Their work had been going badly. In one room, Bell was busy tuning one transmitter after another. In the other room, Watson suddenly noticed that one of the transmitting springs had stopped vibrating. Watson thought it had gotten stuck.

Bell also noticed that something was different. As Watson tried to free the transmission spring, Bell called out for him not to change anything. Bell then came running into the room to see what had happened. In his autobiography, Watson reported what happened next.

> I showed him that it was very simple. The make-and-break points of the transmitter spring I was

Although we know a lot about Alexander Graham Bell, we do not know as much about Thomas Watson, his assistant. This PBS site features a biography of the machinist on its **Thomas A. Watson** Web page.

trying to start had become welded together, so
that when I snapped the spring the circuit had
remained unbroken while that strip of magnetized
steel, by its vibrations over the pole of the magnet,
was generating that marvelous conception of
Bell's—a current of electricity that varied in intensity precisely as the air was varying in density
within hearing distance of the spring.[6]

Bell could hardly believe what had just
occurred. The circuit had transmitted actual tones,
not just on-and-off clicks. As Watson had plucked
one transmitter's metal reed near the electromagnet, Bell had heard an electrically transmitted
twang from the reed in the receiver. If what they
had just witnessed was truly what it seemed, then
they had stumbled on an entirely new discovery in
electricity!

⮕ THE BIG BREAK

To make sure that what they had seen was real,
the two inventors quickly set about repeating the
procedure with every tuning spring in the shop.
They worked late into the night. Sure enough, the
result was always the same. Bell called the varying
current of electricity an undulatory current.

According to Watson, Bell drew up plans for
a device and instructed him to build it the very
next day. Watson wrote, "I was to construct a
wooden plane on which was mounted one of Bell's
harmonic receivers, a tightly stretched parchment

Bell's original sketch for his telephone.

drumhead to the centre of which the free end of the receiver was fashioned; and a mouthpiece arranged to direct the voice against the other end of the drumhead. It was designed to force the reed to follow the vibrations of the voice."[7]

That night Bell sent a letter to his partner Gardiner Greene Hubbard. The letter began "I have accidentally made a discovery of the very greatest importance."[8]

➡ THE TELEPHONE IS BORN

Bell knew that on June 2, 1875, he had made a major breakthrough in his attempt to invent a working telephone. As far as he was concerned, the telephone had been born that day in his lab. But a lot of work still needed to be done before an actual working model of a telephone was in his hands.

Hubbard, however, was not pleased that Bell was spending his time on the telephone. He ordered Bell to continue work on the harmonic telegraph. Hubbard felt the telephone was a very risky proposition, an idea that might never become a reality. The harmonic telegraph, on the other hand, seemed much more of a sure thing—and much more likely to bring profits to Bell's financial backers.

But Bell was intrigued by his accidental discovery and together, he and Watson focused their energy on the telephone. Bell felt guilty about secretly devoting so much time to the telephone.

#5

Salem, Mass
June 2d 1875

Dear Mr Hubbard

N.P.P.   I have accidentally
made a discovery of the very
greatest importance in regard
to the transmitting Instruments.

Indeed so important does
it seem to me that I have
written to the Organ Factory
to delay the completion of
the Reed arrangement until
I have had the opportunity
of consulting you.

I have succeeded today in
transmitting signals without
any battery whatever!

The musical note produced

On June 2, 1875, Bell wrote to Gardiner Greene Hubbard, telling him that he had "accidentally made a discovery of the very greatest importance."

After all, Hubbard and Sanders were paying for his work on the harmonic telegraph.

⊖ Love is in The Air

But Alexander Graham Bell had another reason to feel uneasy. By this time, he realized that he had fallen in love with Hubbard's daughter Mabel. Their relationship was still one of teacher and student, but in Bell's mind, things had changed. He wanted Mabel to become his wife. Bell knew that if she would have him, he would have to ask Hubbard's permission for Mabel's hand in marriage. So Bell could not appear to ignore Hubbard's wishes regarding the harmonic telegraph.

Over the next several months, Bell and Watson continued to work on the harmonic telegraph, but they also struggled to perfect the telephone. They had been able to transmit tones, the sounds of the plucked steel reeds of the tuning forks, over the electric wire. But so far they had not been able to transmit speech.

Meanwhile, Bell became more and more preoccupied with thoughts about Mabel. Finally, he could no longer keep them a secret. He confessed his feelings to his friends, his parents, even to Mabel's parents—to everyone but Mabel herself. On June 30, 1875, Bell wrote to his parents, telling them:

> She is beautiful—accomplished—belongs to one of the best families in the States and has the most

292 Essex St — Salem
Nov. 25th 1875

My dear little girl

You must not scold me this
once if I do sit up for a moment —
even though it is late — to write a
few lines to you.

I little thought when I went to
Cambridge this afternoon — of the surprise
in store for me. You seemed to me
to be drifting away from me — so far away —
with Visible Speech and ever so many things
between — and I almost despaired of
ever reaching you.

I little thought how near you
were. I can scarcely believe now that
you really and truly love me — and
that you will be my wife. I am
afraid to go to sleep lest I should find
it all a dream — so I shall lie awake
and think of you.

It is so cold and selfish living
all for oneself! A man is only half a
man who has no one to love and to cherish.
"A delicate hot-house plant" (like you) is
far more valuable to me than one that
can stand the storms and buffets of this rude
world alone. It will be my pride and
delight — Mabel — to protect and to love
you. Don't go from me any more.

May God guide us both so that
we may be a comfort and support to
each other. Yours and yours only

Alec.

Miss Mabel G. Hubbard
Brattle St — Cambridge

▲ Bell had a big year in 1875—professionally and personally. He fell in love with Mabel Hubbard and she fell in love with him. In a letter to her on November 25, Bell spoke of how happy he was that she returned his affections, writing, "I am afraid to go to sleep lest I should find it all a dream—so I shall lie awake and think of you."

affectionate disposition that it has been my lot to come across. Her deafness I felt to be a great bar. Her youth too—(she is only now 17 and a half)— rendered it unlikely that she should reciprocate [return] my feelings. . . . One difficulty I knew that I should encounter was the fact of my looking so much older than I am. Not one of the family thought me less than 36 (!) until I informed them a day or two before I spoke to Mrs. Hubbard of my being only 28.[9]

Though Bell was distracted, he and Watson continued their work. Unfortunately, his health began to suffer from his emotional turmoil. Finally, he poured out his heart in a letter to Mabel. She received the news with mixed feelings.

⮕ LOVE CONNECTION

On August 30, 1875, Mabel responded. "Perhaps it is best we should not meet awhile now, and that when we do meet we should not speak of love. It is too sacred and delicate a subject to be talked about much and till I know what it means myself I cannot understand or fully sympathize with the feeling. Only if you ever again need my friendly help and sympathy it is yours."[10] Bell was heartened by Mabel's letter, even if her words were not exactly what he wanted to hear.

The following month, in September, Bell began writing up his ideas about multiple telegraphy and the basics of telephony, without ever using the word "telephone." He completed this written work in October. Meanwhile, Mrs. Hubbard had grown more supportive of Bell's interest in her daughter.

Thanksgiving Day, November 25, 1875, would give Bell much to be thankful for. It was Mabel's eighteenth birthday and she celebrated by becoming engaged to Bell. He was overjoyed. He wrote to his parents, "Mabel has today trusted herself to me and promised to be my wife. . . . My heart is too full to allow me to write much to you tonight."[11]

⮕ PATENT NUMBER 174,465

In January 1876, Bell rented a new work space at 5 Exeter Place in Boston and he and Watson set up their new laboratory. One day, Hubbard told Bell the time had come to file for a patent for the harmonic telegraph and the telephone. By this time, Hubbard had become convinced that Bell's inventions could be hugely successful and he was concerned that unless the patent was secured soon, Elisha Gray would beat them to it. Bell would lose all chance at fame and fortune, and Hubbard and Sanders would miss the chance to financially benefit from their investment. But Bell was not ready: He still had more work to do on his telephone.

Hubbard soon learned that Gray was very close to filing for a patent for a telephone, so he decided to take matters into his own hands. On February 14, 1876, at 11:00 A.M., Hubbard filed for the patent in Bell's name without telling the inventor.

The application included the descriptive material Bell had written the previous fall.

That same morning, just two hours earlier, Gray had filed his own application. But Gray had only filed a caveat, the right to file for a patent at a later date. Gray could have converted his caveat into a patent. But he did not do so. At the time, neither Gray nor Bell had a working model of a telephone. When Hubbard informed Bell that he had filed for a patent in Bell's name, the young inventor became nervous. He might get a patent, but what would he do if he could not make his telephone work?

On March 7, 1876, patent number 174,465 was granted to Alexander Graham Bell for "Improvements in Telegraphy." This patent has often been called the most valuable patent ever issued. In it, Bell never mentioned the word "telephone." But thanks to his clear description of the various components of his telephone and their function, it was now impossible for anyone else to design a working telephone without infringing Bell's work.

⮕ Success at Last

Now that he had secured a patent, Bell knew that he simply had to make the telephone work and he had no choice but to do so quickly. If he could not produce a working telephone, he could be testimony whereof I have hereunto signed name this 20th day of January A.D. 1876

Witnesses
Thomas E. Barry   Alex. Graham Bell
P.W. Richards

State of Massachusetts
Suffolk County   }ss.

Alexander Graham Bell — the above named petitioner being duly sworn deposes and says that he verily believes himself to be the original and first inventor of the Improvements in Telegraphy

described and claimed in the foregoing specification; that he does not know and does not believe that the same was ever before known or used; and that he is a native of Great Britain, and has declared his intention of becoming a citizen of the United States.

Thomas E. Barry   }   Alex. Graham Bell
P.W. Richards   } witnesses

Sworn to and subscribed before me this 20th day of January A.D. 1876

Thomas E. Barry
Notary Public

6½ 15   340 found guilty of fraud. Bell and Watson threw themselves into their work with a tremendous drive to succeed.

The sounds from the transmitter were still unclear at the receiver end of the wire. So the two inventors tinkered with anything and everything. At times, it seemed as though they were grasping at straws.

On March 10, 1876, Bell and Watson were hard at work in their laboratory. That afternoon, they prepared to test their latest setup. Bell was in one room, leaning over the transmitter. In another room, separated by two closed doors, Watson waited with the receiver pressed against his ear.

➔ LOUD AND CLEAR

In his notebook, Bell described what happened next: "I then shouted into M [the mouthpiece] the following sentence: 'Mr. Watson—Come here—I want to see you.' To my delight he came and declared that he had heard and understood what I said. I asked him to repeat the words. He answered 'You said—Mr. Watson—come here—I want to see you.'"[12] With those simple words, Bell and Watson had the world's first telephone conversation.

Bell and Watson were thrilled—they had finally succeeded in making the telephone work.

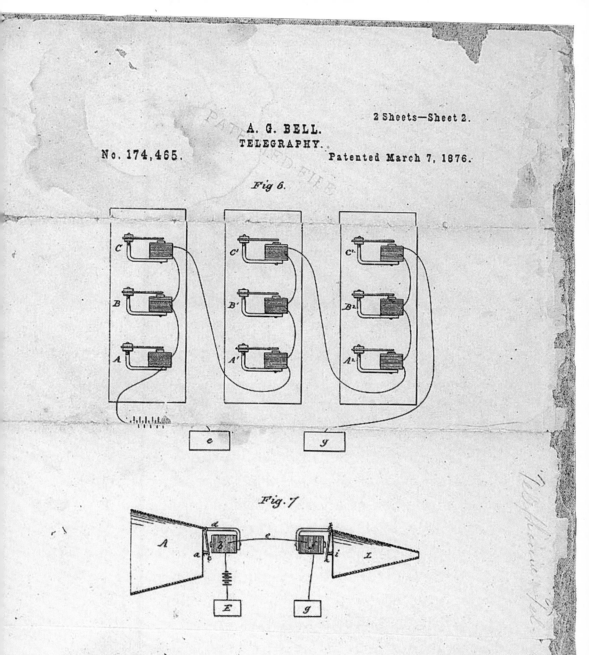

A. G. BELL.
TELEGRAPHY.

No. 174,465. Patented March 7, 1876.

Fig 6.

Fig. 7

Witnesses

Inventor:
a. Graham Bell

A simple drawing for a complex device that revolutionized the world: This is Bell's drawing of his telephone, which was part of his patent application.

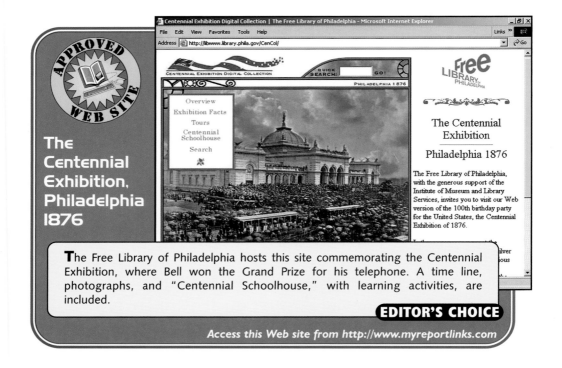

The
Centennial
Exhibition,
Philadelphia
1876

The Free Library of Philadelphia hosts this site commemorating the Centennial Exhibition, where Bell won the Grand Prize for his telephone. A time line, photographs, and "Centennial Schoolhouse," with learning activities, are included.

EDITOR'S CHOICE

Access this Web site from http://www.myreportlinks.com

Later that day, Bell wrote to his father, "This is a great day with me. I feel that I have at last struck the solution of a great problem—and the day is coming when telegraph wires will be laid on to houses just like water or gas—and friends converse with each other without leaving home."[13]

THE CENTENNIAL EXHIBITION

In the spring of 1876, America was gearing up for the Centennial Exhibition. The event, a celebration of the nation's one hundredth birthday, was to take place in Philadelphia in June. Among the most important exhibits would be those devoted to the latest developments in science and technology. The exhibits would be judged by some of the nation's leading scientists. The judging of electric exhibits was scheduled for June 23 through June 26.

This was certainly an exciting time in the life of Alexander Graham Bell. He had made an incredible breakthrough in telecommunications technology. He was aware that his invention had the potential to have a huge and lasting impact in the world. Hubbard, of course, expected Bell to show his telephone at the Centennial Exhibition. But Bell still felt his telephone was not yet ready

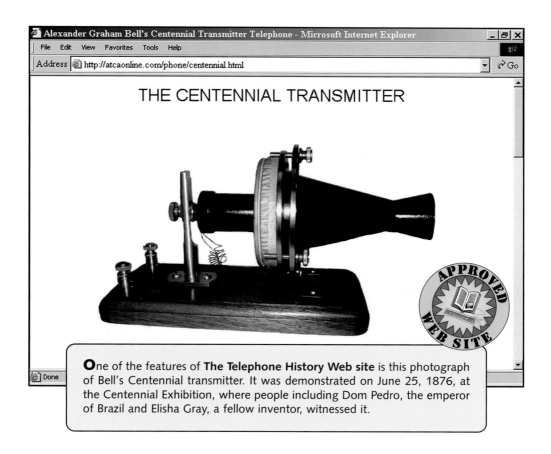

Alexander Graham Bell's Centennial Transmitter Telephone - Microsoft Internet Explorer

File   Edit   View   Favorites   Tools   Help

Address http://atcaonline.com/phone/centennial.html

THE CENTENNIAL TRANSMITTER

One of the features of **The Telephone History Web site** is this photograph of Bell's Centennial transmitter. It was demonstrated on June 25, 1876, at the Centennial Exhibition, where people including Dom Pedro, the emperor of Brazil and Elisha Gray, a fellow inventor, witnessed it.

for such an important exhibition. More work was needed to perfect it, and this would take time. Bell was also intimidated by the fact that the nation's leading scientists would be judging the exhibits.

To make matters worse, Bell was feeling guilty about his students, whom he felt he had neglected in the rush to finish the telephone. He now intended to dedicate more time to them and he was still committed to using the Visible Speech system to teach them to speak.

⇒ HESITANT, THEN HAILED

But Hubbard insisted that Bell show his telephone at the Centennial Exhibition. Mabel, now Bell's fiancée, agreed with her father. She urged Bell to go to Philadelphia in June. Bell had planned to demonstrate the Visible Speech system at the Massachusetts education exhibit. But he had waited too long to enter his inventions in the science section, which was already filled. So Bell had no choice but to set up his telephone display at his Visible Speech booth.

Early in the exhibition, Bell's telephone display was not drawing much attention. It was set up far from the other scientific exhibits. So Bell wandered over to the science area. There he stood in the audience while Elisha Gray demonstrated his multiple telegraph. The crowd was impressed, and the judges awarded Gray a medal.

It was late in the day. Bell had all but given up hope that anyone would pay attention to his invention. But then a familiar voice cried out a greeting. It was Dom Pedro, the emperor of Brazil. He had visited Bell in Boston to learn about Visible Speech. He followed Bell back to his booth to see the telephone. Along the way, they rounded up any of the judges they came across.

Back at the booth, Bell demonstrated his telephone for the emperor, the judges, and the small crowd that had gathered. In the crowd was Sir William Thomson, at the time the world's leading physicist. He was visiting the Centennial Exhibition from England. To Bell's great relief, the telephone worked, and those who witnessed it believed they had witnessed a miracle. Sir William Thomson hailed the telephone as the most marvelous invention he had seen in America. The Centennial Exhibition judges awarded Bell their Grand Prize.

How the Telephone Changed the World

CHAPTER 5

By the time Alexander Graham Bell turned thirty in 1877, he had already achieved great international fame for inventing the telephone. And he topped that professional milestone with a personal one: on July 11, he married Mabel Hubbard. For their honeymoon, the happy couple went first to Niagara Falls and then to England and Scotland. In England, Bell demonstrated his telephone for Great Britain's Queen Victoria at the royal palace.

As they were traveling, Bell, ever the inventor, kept trying to understand how everything worked. In Scotland, he watched seagulls, trying to understand how they flew. In the back of his mind, he envisioned flying machines. Later he used up all of the couple's sugar cubes—he dropped them into the water to try to find out where the bubbles came from. Mabel marveled at the way her husband's mind worked.

What a man my husband is! I am perfectly bewildered at the number and size of the ideas with which his head is crammed. . . . Flying machines to which telephones and torpedoes are to be attached occupy the first place just now from observations of seagulls. . . . Every now and then he comes out with 'the flying machine has quite changed its shape in a quarter of an hour' or 'the segar-shape is dismissed to the limbo of useless things.'. . . Then he goes climbing about the rocks and forming theories on the origin of cliffs and caves. . . . Then he comes home and watches sugar bubbles.[1]

When Mr. and Mrs. Bell returned to the United States, they lived in Washington, D.C. Years later, Bell bought land near Baddeck, Cape Breton Island, in Nova Scotia, Canada. There he built a magnificent estate on a hill overlooking the sea. The scenery reminded Bell of his beloved Scotland. He called the home Beinn Bhreagh, Gaelic for "beautiful mountain." There he and Mabel and their two daughters would spend many happy summers.

Bell's invention of the telephone had brought him more money than most people ever dream of. The first important step in building that fortune was the creation of the Bell Telephone Company.

➔ THE BELL TELEPHONE COMPANY

On July 9, 1877, Bell, Watson, Hubbard, and Sanders formed the Bell Telephone Company. During the first period of its growth, the company competed with the Western Union Telegraph Company for dominance in

In an 1885 photograph, Bell and his wife Mabel pose with daughters Elsie and Marian, also known as Daisy.

telecommunications. Needing additional investors, on March 25, 1878, Bell wrote to a group of businessmen in England. He hoped to persuade them about the advantages of telephony over telegraphy.

> The telephone may be briefly described as an electrical contrivance for reproducing in distant places the tones and articulation of a speaker's voice, so that conversation can be carried on by word of mouth, between persons in different rooms, in different streets, in different towns.
>
> The great advantage it possesses over every other form of electrical apparatus consists in the fact that it requires no skill to operate the instrument. All other telegraph machines produce signals which require to be translated by experts, and such instruments are therefore extremely limited in their

▲ *Beinn Bhreagh, the Bell home on Cape Breton Island, Nova Scotia. The Bells were drawn to this spot in the province whose name translates as "New Scotland" in part because it reminded Bell of his homeland.*

application, but the telephone actually speaks, and for this reason it can be utilized for nearly every purpose for which speech is employed.[2]

⇒ TECHNICAL PROBLEMS

From nearly the first days of the Bell Telephone Company's existence, Bell and his lawyers became involved in lawsuits over patents. Other inventors claimed to have invented the telephone or various technological improvements for it. These included Johann Philipp Reis, Elisha Gray, and Thomas Edison. The last court fight ended in 1893. Bell, thanks to the brilliance of his invention and the timely securing of a patent, was able to successfully defend his claims on the telephone against any and all challengers.

Before the telephone could become a practical means of communication, many technical problems had to be solved. Bell's first telephone system consisted of only two telephones connected by a wire. Bell had to devise a way to improve telephone transmission and to expand this simple system into a network. Wires were needed to connect homes and businesses to other homes and businesses on other parts of the street. Then connections were needed to other streets in other parts of the city and to other cities in other parts of the country. The network would require a switching system in order to function. Bell also worked on improving the telephone's

American Heritage's online magazine features an article about the race between Bell and others to obtain a patent for the telephone.

Access this Web site from http://www.myreportlinks.com

sound quality so that the voice heard by a listener sounded like the voice of the speaker.

➡ THE PHONE'S EVOLUTION

Bell and Watson continued trying to improve their telephone. On January 30, 1877, Bell was granted a patent for an electromagnetic telephone. Its transmitter and receiver used steel diaphragms and a call bell. While Bell and Watson were making progress, other inventors, including Thomas Edison, were also busy inventing ways to make telephone transmission better. On April 27, 1877, Edison filed for a patent on a carbon transmitter. He was granted the patent in 1892, after years of lawsuits against Emile Berliner, a scientist working with Bell. Eventually, both Edison's carbon transmitter and Bell's electromagnetic receiver were used together in the Bell system.

→ BELL TELEPHONE GROWS UP

Meanwhile, the Bell Telephone Company grew by leaps and bounds. The first switchboard began operating in Boston in the spring of 1877. A switchboard is a panel on which electric switches are mounted and arranged so that electric circuits can be connected, combined, and controlled. These circuits were manually operated (which is how the term operator came into being). The first operators were young boys who were often rude to callers. By 1910, women, who were thought to be more polite—and who also turned out to be faster at making the switchboard connections—filled most operator positions.[3]

In 1878, the first telephone exchange, a central office where telephone lines are connected, began operating in New Haven, Connecticut. The first telephone directory was also printed there. That same year, the famous writer Mark Twain had a telephone installed in his home in Hartford, Connecticut. Twain, who loved new technology, had persuaded his boss at the *Hartford Courant* to hook up a direct line from the newspaper office to his home. The telephone quickly became a good target for Twain's particular style of humor. As the telephone was being set up, Twain said, "The voice carries entirely too far as it is. If Bell had invented a muffler or a gag he would have done a real service. . . . Put the thing near the window, so that I can get rid of it easily."[4]

By 1880, there were 47,900 telephones in the United States. By 1881, there were more than 132,000. Telephone communication was limited to calls within the same city, but the system continued to develop rapidly. In 1885, the Bell Telephone Company created the American Telephone and Telegraph Company (AT&T) to offer long-distance services between cities. In 1892, Bell made a phone call from New York City to Chicago,

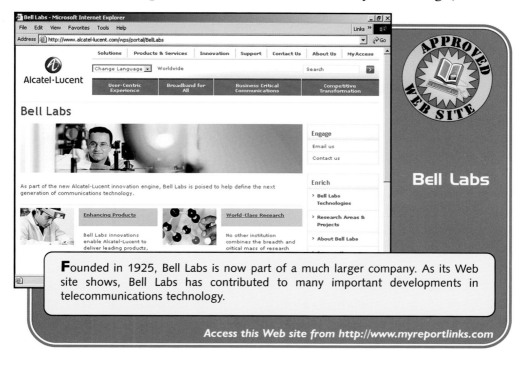

Founded in 1925, Bell Labs is now part of a much larger company. As its Web site shows, Bell Labs has contributed to many important developments in telecommunications technology.

Access this Web site from http://www.myreportlinks.com

An 1886 portrait of Bell, ten years after he made the world's first telephone call.

as his company began long-distance telephone service between those two cities.

⇒ Connecting the Coasts

In 1915, coast-to-coast telephone service began in the United States. On the afternoon of January 25 of that year, Alexander Graham Bell picked up a telephone in New York City. He placed a call to Thomas Watson, who was in San Francisco, California. The nation's first transcontinental phone call consisted of the following exchange:

Bell: "Hoy, hoy, Mr. Watson are you there? Do you hear me?"

Watson: "Yes, Mr. Bell, I hear you perfectly. Do you hear me well?"

Bell: "Yes, your voice is perfectly distinct. It is as clear as if you were here in New York instead of being more than three thousand miles away. You remember, Mr. Watson, that evening, thirty-eight years ago when we conversed through a telephone on a real line for the first time?"

Watson: "Yes, indeed, that line was two miles long, running from Boston to Cambridge. You were overjoyed at the success of the experiment."[5]

Then both men hung up their latest state-of-the-art telephones. They connected replicas of their original 1875 telephone and had the following conversation:

Bell: "I am now talking through an exact duplicate of the first telephone which was made in June 1875. Can you hear me?"

Watson: "I hear perfectly, though less distinctly than with the other, of course."

Bell: "Mr. Watson, come here, I want you."

Watson: "It would take me a week to get to you this time."[6]

By 1921, 13 percent of Americans had telephones. Suddenly, people were just a phone call away from friends and relatives, even those on opposite sides of the country. The telephone had quickly become an essential part of life.

⇒ BELL'S LEGACY

Alexander Graham Bell died on August 2, 1922, at Beinn Bhreagh, Nova Scotia. Thanks to his telephone, the world had become a smaller place. At the time of Bell's death, there were more than 10 million telephones in North America. Four years after Bell's death, the world shrank even more. In 1926, Bell Labs and the British Post Office engineered the first two-way telephone conversation across the Atlantic Ocean. Then on January 7, 1927, the first commercial transatlantic telephone call took place between New York City and London.

The telephone revolutionized communication. Today, thanks to the cell phone, we can now reach

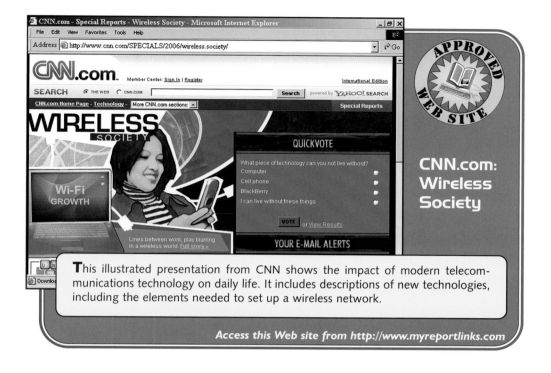

This illustrated presentation from CNN shows the impact of modern telecommunications technology on daily life. It includes descriptions of new technologies, including the elements needed to set up a wireless network.

Access this Web site from http://www.myreportlinks.com

others and be reached any time of day or night, no matter where we are.

Business could not operate in today's world without modern telecommunications. Every advance in telecommunications technology has brought about greater efficiencies in the corporate world. Technological progress has also lowered the costs of telephone service. The most recent development, VOIP (voice over the Internet protocol), will lower costs even more. All of these technologies, which we tend to take for granted now, were made possible by the work of Alexander Graham Bell.

BELL'S OTHER INVENTIONS

Alexander Graham Bell is most remembered for having invented the telephone. And that single contribution would have been more than enough to earn him lasting fame and honor. But throughout his life, Bell remained curious about the world and how it worked, and he never stopped trying to improve things or invent entirely new devices that might make the world better. In 1880, he established the Volta Laboratory in Washington, D.C., where he could conduct experiments. At the time he said that an inventor "can no more help inventing than he can help thinking or breathing."[1]

Bell also described his motivation in a speech he delivered in 1891: "An inventor is a man who looks around upon the world and is not content with things as they are; he wants to improve whatever he sees; he wants to benefit the world; he is haunted by an idea; the spirit of inventiveness possesses him, seeing material-

CHAPTER

6

➔ Bell and Helen Keller: From Darkness Into Light

Bell's work with deaf people and his desire to teach them speech remained an important part of his life, even though that work was overshadowed by his invention of the tele-phone. As Bell later remarked, "One would think I had never done anything worthwhile but the telephone. That is because it is a money-making invention. It is a pity so many people make money the criterion of success. I wish my experience had resulted in enabling the deaf to speak with less diffi-culty. That would have made me truly happy."[3] In 1890, Bell founded the American Association for the Teaching of Speech to the Deaf. It was later renamed the A. G. Bell Association for the Deaf.

In the summer of 1886, Captain Arthur Keller traveled from his home in Alabama to Washing-ton, D.C., to meet Bell. Keller brought his six-year-old daugh-ter, Helen, with him. An illness when she was only nineteen months old had left her deaf, blind, and unable to speak. Bell had been recommended to Keller as a man deeply committed to the education of deaf children, and Keller hoped Bell would

Although Bell is best known for inventing the telephone, he was first a teacher of the deaf, and it was in that capacity that he came to know Helen Keller. Here, Bell "speaks" to Keller, surrounded by family and friends, through finger spelling.

be able to help his daughter. Years later, in her autobiography, Helen Keller described that first meeting with Bell and what it meant to her: "Child as I was, I at once felt the tenderness and sympathy which endeared Dr. Bell to so many hearts . . . But I did not dream that that interview would be the door through which I should pass from darkness into light, from isolation to friendship, companionship, knowledge, love."[4]

⊜ Fast Friends

Bell helped Captain Keller find a teacher for Helen. The teacher, a young woman named Anne Mansfield Sullivan, eventually found a way to teach Helen to speak, read, and write. Bell remained a devoted and supportive friend to Helen Keller for as long as he lived. He offered her financial help and educational guidance whenever necessary.

Like Bell, Helen Keller had always been very curious about the world around her. She had a thirst for knowledge, and Bell was happy to take the time to explain things to her. One day, he tried to convey to her what his invention of the telephone meant to the world. While they were walking, Bell placed Helen's hand on a telephone pole. She could feel vibrations and asked if it always hummed. Bell said yes and explained that the wires "sang of life and death, war and

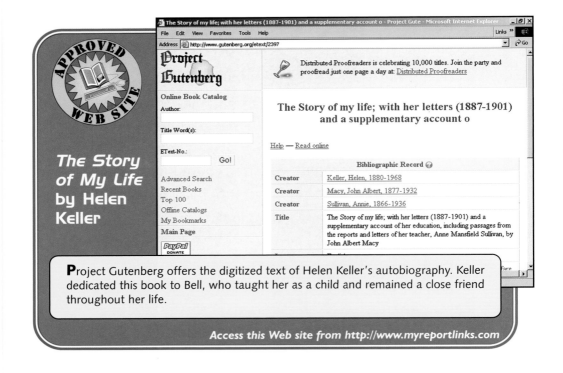

The Story of my life; with her letters (1887-1901) and a supplementary account o - Project Gute - Microsoft Internet Explorer

File   Edit   View   Favorites   Tools   Help

Links »

Address http://www.gutenberg.org/etext/2397

Project Gutenberg

Distributed Proofreaders is celebrating 10,000 titles. Join the party and proofread just one page a day at: Distributed Proofreaders

Online Book Catalog

Author:

The Story of my life; with her letters (1887-1901) and a supplementary account o

Title Word(s):

Help — Read online

EText-No.:   Go!

	Bibliographic Record
Creator	Keller, Helen, 1880-1968
Creator	Macy, John Albert, 1877-1932
Creator	Sullivan, Annie, 1866-1936
Title	The Story of my life; with her letters (1887-1901) and a supplementary account of her education, including passages from the reports and letters of her teacher, Anne Mansfield Sullivan, by John Albert Macy

Advanced Search
Recent Books
Top 100
Offline Catalogs
My Bookmarks
Main Page

PayPal DONATE

The Story of My Life by Helen Keller

Project Gutenberg offers the digitized text of Helen Keller's autobiography. Keller dedicated this book to Bell, who taught her as a child and remained a close friend throughout her life.

Access this Web site from http://www.myreportlinks.com

finance, fear and joy, failure and success, that they pierced the barriers of space and touched mind to mind throughout the world."[5]

Then Bell explained how voices are carried over the wires. He said, "Those copper wires up there are carrying the news of birth and death, war and finance, failure and success, from station to station around the world."[6]

When Helen Keller's autobiography was published, the dedication read "To Alexander Graham Bell, who has taught the deaf to speak and enabled the listening ear to hear speech from the Atlantic to the Rockies, I dedicate this Story of My Life."[7]

⇒ THE AUDIOMETER

As his friendship with Helen Keller showed, Bell never lost his devotion to those who were hard of hearing or deaf. And in 1879, he invented the audiometer, a device that tested a patient's range of hearing from the highest to lowest frequencies. The audiometer sent a series of different tones to a small speaker held against the patient's ear. At each frequency, the volume of the transmitted tones kept getting lower. The patient would record the point at which he or she could no longer hear the tone.

To measure the intensity or volume of the sounds transmitted by the audiometer, Bell invented a unit of sound. Named the "bel" in honor of its inventor, this unit is still used today to measure the volume of sounds from speakers and amplifiers. Usually, the sounds are measured in decibels (dB), or tenths of a bel.

⇒ THE PHOTOPHONE

Bell's photophone was based on an entirely different type of technology than his earlier telephone. The photophone transmitted sound over a beam of light.

Bell and an assistant, Charles Sumner Tainter, developed a light-sensitive selenium cell. A selenium cell is an insulated strip of the element selenium, which is sensitive to light. They placed

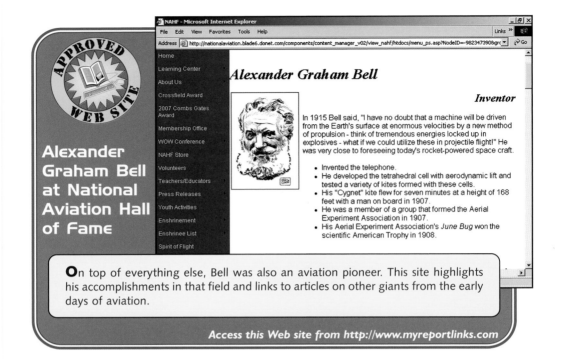

APPROVED WEB SITE

Alexander Graham Bell at National Aviation Hall of Fame

NAHF - Microsoft Internet Explorer

File Edit View Favorites Tools Help

Links

Address http://nationalaviation.blade6.donet.com/components/content_manager_v02/view_nahf/htdocs/menu_ps.asp?NodeID=-9823473908grc

Go

Home
Learning Center
About Us
Crossfield Award
2007 Combs Gates Award
Membership Office
WOW Conference
NAHF Store
Volunteers
Teachers/Educators
Press Releases
Youth Activities
Enshrinement
Enshrinee List
Spirit of Flight

Alexander Graham Bell

Inventor

In 1915 Bell said, "I have no doubt that a machine will be driven from the Earth's surface at enormous velocities by a new method of propulsion - think of tremendous energies locked up in explosives - what if we could utilize these in projectile flight!" He was very close to foreseeing today's rocket-powered space craft.

- Invented the telephone.
- He developed the tetrahedral cell with aerodynamic lift and tested a variety of kites formed with these cells.
- His "Cygnet" kite flew for seven minutes at a height of 168 feet with a man on board in 1907.
- He was a member of a group that formed the Aerial Experiment Association in 1907.
- His Aerial Experiment Association's *June Bug* won the scientific American Trophy in 1908.

On top of everything else, Bell was also an aviation pioneer. This site highlights his accomplishments in that field and links to articles on other giants from the early days of aviation.

Access this Web site from http://www.myreportlinks.com

the cell in a telephone circuit. They then used a system of lenses to bounce a beam of sunlight reflected from a voice-vibrated mirror onto the selenium cell. The voice varied the intensity of the reflected beam by distorting the surface of the mirror. This caused the resistance of the selenium cell to vary. And this in turn made the battery current rise and fall, which was necessary for telephonic speech. Many years later, that technology led to the development of today's fiber optics and laser communication systems. (Fiber optics are thin, flexible fibers of transparent glass or plastic that transmit light.) Bell's discoveries proved helpful to engineers who had to figure out how to transmit voice signals over beams of light within fiber-optic cables.

Bell was thrilled by this new system of tele-communication. On February 26, 1880, he sent a letter to his father expressing his excitement.

> *I have heard articulate speech produced by sunlight! I have heard a ray of the sun laugh and cough and sing!* . . . I have been able to *hear a shadow,* and I have even perceived by ear *the passage of a cloud across the sun's disk.* . . . Can Imagination picture what the future of this invention is to be! . . . We

http://fi.edu/case_files/bell/medium/acceptance.jpg - Microsoft Internet Explorer

File   Edit   View   Favorites   Tools   Help

Address http://fi.edu/case_files/bell/medium/acceptance.jpg

Mr. and Mrs. Graham Bell have pleasure in accepting the invitation of the Franklin Institute to attend a stated meeting to be held on the evening of May 15 at eight o'clock.

APPROVED WEB SITE

In 1912, the Franklin Institute awarded Bell the Elliott Cresson Medal in the field of engineering for "Electrical Transmission of Articulate Speech." This note from the Bells is their acceptance of the invitation to attend that award ceremony. **The Case Files: Alexander Graham Bell,** a site from the institute, explores Bell's life and the science behind his inventions.

EDITOR'S CHOICE

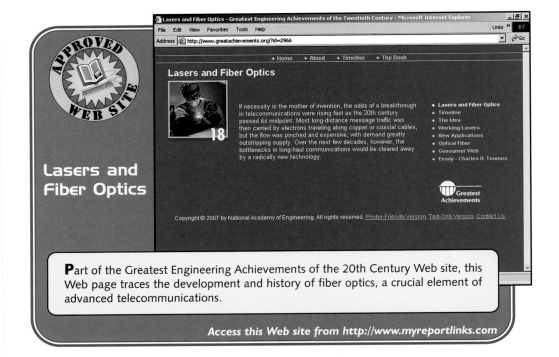

◆ Home   ◆ About   ◆ Timeline   ◆ The Book

Lasers and Fiber Optics

If necessity is the mother of invention, the odds of a breakthrough in telecommunications were rising fast as the 20th century passed its midpoint. Most long-distance message traffic was then carried by electrons traveling along copper or coaxial cables, but the flow was pinched and expensive, with demand greatly outstripping supply. Over the next few decades, however, the bottlenecks in long-haul communications would be cleared away by a radically new technology.

◆ Lasers and Fiber Optics
◆ Timeline
◆ The Idea
◆ Working Lasers
◆ New Applications
◆ Optical Fiber
◆ Gossamer Web
◆ Essay - Charles H. Townes

Greatest
Achievements

Part of the Greatest Engineering Achievements of the 20th Century Web site, this Web page traces the development and history of fiber optics, a crucial element of advanced telecommunications.

Access this Web site from http://www.myreportlinks.com

may talk by light to any visible distance without any conducting wire. . . . In warfare the electric communications of an army could neither be cut nor tapped. On the ocean communication may be carried on . . . between . . . vessels . . . and light-houses may be identified by the sound of their lights. In general science, discoveries will be made by the Photophone that are undreamed of just now. . . . The twinkling stars may yet be recognized by characteristic sounds, and storms and sun-spots be detected in the sun.[8]

Bell patented the photophone in 1880, and despite his early optimism, it was not a very successful invention. The quality of the sound transmission was poor, and Bell never perfected it.

It was also not practical. Its use was limited to "line-of-sight" transmission, and only on sunny days. However, the science behind it was solid, and Bell's prediction that the ability to transmit sound over light would be important did come true.

⇒ BELL TRIES TO SAVE THE PRESIDENT

Two of Bell's later inventions resulted from tragedy in the summer of 1881. On July 2, President James Garfield was shot in the waiting room of the Baltimore and Potomac train station in Washington, D.C. Doctors desperately tried to find the bullet in his body. They probed the president's wounds with bare fingers and unsterilized instruments, which was common practice at the time—X-ray machines had not been invented yet. Not able to locate the bullet, they contacted Bell, hoping he might know of some way to detect it.

Within three weeks of the assassination attempt on the president, Bell finished building a metal detector based on an induction balance, a device that had been invented by Bell's friend David Hughes to correct interference over a telephone line. Bell had begun experimenting with the design of a metal detector even before Garfield was shot. The president's shooting propelled Bell to move from design to construction. He first tested his device on thirty Civil War veterans who, more than fifteen years after the end of the war, still had

WASHINGTON, D. C.—THE ATTEMPTED ASSASSINATION OF THE PRESIDENT—THE DISCOVERY OF THE LOCATION

NEW YORK.—FIRST CELEBRATION OF PRESIDENT GARFIELD'S RECOVERY—THE DISPLAY OF FIREWORKS AT FORT GREENE, BROOKLYN,
AUGUST 4TH.—SEE PAGE 411.

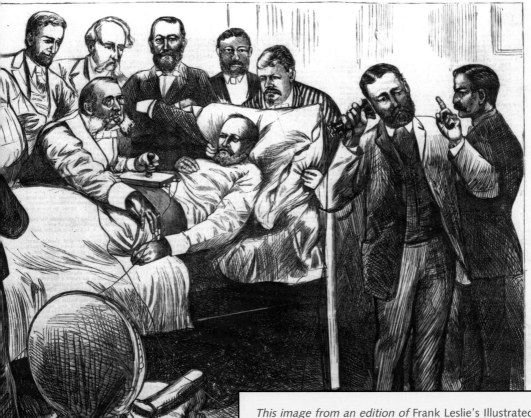

This image from an edition of Frank Leslie's Illustrated Newspaper, a popular periodical of the time, captures events related to the assassination of President Garfield. The top print shows Bell attempting to find the bullet using an induction balance.

LET BY MEANS OF PROFESSOR BELL'S INDUCTION-BALANCE.—FROM A SKETCH BY WILLIAM A. SKINKLE.—SEE PAGE 411.

RSEY.—THE SEASIDE SABBATH-SCHOOL ASSEMBLY AT ASBURY PARK, AUGUST 2D-12TH—THE EVENING PRAISE-SERVICE IN THE PAVILION ON THE BEACH, AUGUST 7TH.—FROM A SKETCH BY A STAFF ARTIST.—SEE PAGE 415.

bullets in their bodies. In each case, Bell's metal detector located the bullet. But when Bell tried the device on Garfield, it failed to find the bullet. Bell tried twice more, but each time he failed.

Bell returned to Garfield's bedside on August 1 with an improved version of the metal detector. This time, his device located the bullet near Garfield's spine. Unfortunately, the doctors were not able to remove it. Even worse, their probing introduced an infection to Garfield's wounds, which led to blood poisoning. The president died on September 19.

Too late, Bell realized why his metal detector had not worked the first time. The metal frame and coil springs on Garfield's bed had interfered with the functioning of the metal detector. Sadly, and incorrectly, some Washington newspapers blamed Bell for the president's death.

⇒ AN INVENTION BORN OF PERSONAL LOSS

While Bell was trying to save President Garfield with his device, a personal tragedy struck. Bell's wife, Mabel, who was pregnant, had gone to Boston to be with her relatives while her husband was occupied trying to perfect his metal detector. Mabel Bell gave birth to a son on August 15, but the child, named Edward, died of lung failure within hours of his birth. Bell was overcome with grief—and guilt because he had not been there to help his wife or his newborn son. He immediately went to work in his laboratory to try to invent something that might save others stricken with similar breathing problems.

The result was an invention Bell called the vacuum jacket. The metal jacket fit tightly around a patient's chest. A pump was attached to air pockets in the jacket. When air was pumped into the jacket, it forced the patient to breathe out. When it sucked air out, the resulting vacuum caused the patient's chest to expand, allowing the patient to breathe. Eventually, Bell's vacuum jacket respirator led other inventors to develop the iron lung, which became an important aid in the mid-twentieth century to people suffering from polio.

EXPERIMENTS IN THE AIR

In addition to all of his other interests, Bell had long been fascinated by the idea of manned flight. Ever since he was a child, he had marveled at the flight of birds and had wondered whether humans too might be able to fly, with a little help. In 1878, he drew sketches of a flying machine. Several years later, he began experimenting with kites of many different shapes. His goal was to design a kite capable of lifting a human into the air.

In 1891, Bell discovered the strength of the tetrahedron. The pyramid-shaped tetrahedron is made of rods joined to form four triangular sides.

1892 Sept. 14 —

Exp. 1   Old ~~great~~ Vac...
England for me —
received by Mr. Mc...
at King's College — ...
in order for tr...
seemed to have to...
it has been remo...
substituted — 1½

John McKillop ...
to succeed perfectly
John McKillop sto...
effort to breathe —
moved to and fro...

ed — at VB. Rob.

…n jacket made in
many years ago — and
…ely from Prof. Yeo —
…ndow — has been put
…l. Brass pipe attached
…small chamber — to
…ed and larger tube
…ch diam.

John McKillop

Bellows… …
…se …new tube

…ed to experiment — …seemed
…W. Ellis worked bellows.
…I think he made zero
…yet a piece of paper was
…when held in front of

Tetrahedron cells can be combined to form almost any shape. Bell used tetrahedrons to build giant box kites. In 1906, one of Bell's tetrahedron kites lifted two men off the ground.

In 1893, Bell predicted that within ten years, the problems of people flying through the air would be solved, and he also believed that this would revolutionize travel. In 1896, Bell and Samuel Langley flew an unmanned steam-powered flying machine a distance of more than 3,000 feet (914 meters). Only seven years later, on December 17, 1903, the Wright brothers made the world's first manned powered flight in an airplane.

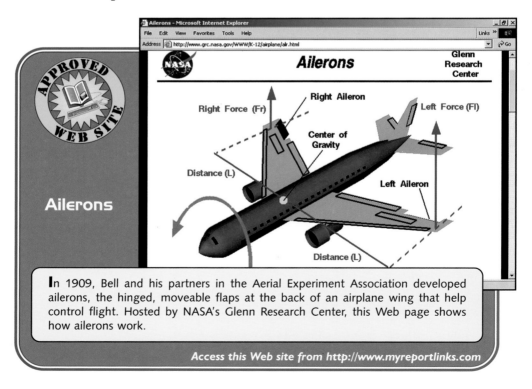

In 1909, Bell and his partners in the Aerial Experiment Association developed ailerons, the hinged, moveable flaps at the back of an airplane wing that help control flight. Hosted by NASA's Glenn Research Center, this Web page shows how ailerons work.

Access this Web site from http://www.myreportlinks.com

In 1907, Bell and four partners formed the Aerial Experiment Association (AEA) in Nova Scotia. In 1909, their fourth experimental plane, the *Silver Dart,* made the first engine-powered flight in Canada. While experimenting with flight, Bell invented the aileron to help control the flight of a plane. Ailerons are hinged movable flaps on the back side of each wing.

⇒EXPERIMENTS ON WATER

During the last years of his life, Bell experimented with hydrofoil boats. A hydrofoil boat has wings (foils) that fly in the water (*hydro* is a root word meaning "water"). A hydrofoil is capable of moving much faster than other boats. Its hull (frame or body) is raised, and only its wings glide through the water. Bell's experience with flying gave him ideas for improving the performance of the hydrofoil.

In 1908, Bell and an assistant, Casey Baldwin, studied the work of the Italian inventor Enrico Forlanini who developed the first hydrofoil boat. Bell and Baldwin began testing their own hydrofoil models. In 1910, Bell and Baldwin traveled to Italy to meet Forlanini. He took them for a ride on Lake Maggiore in his boat. Bell and Baldwin were impressed at the smoothness of the ride. The following year, they built their first hydrofoil, the HD-1. During the following years

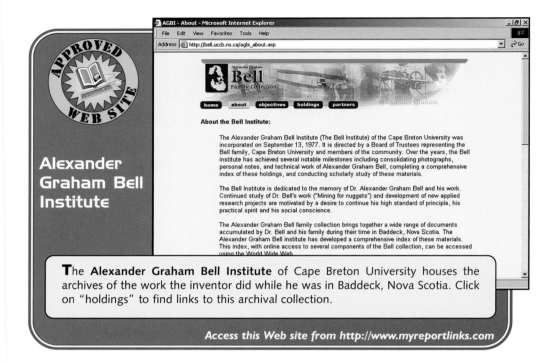

Alexander Graham Bell Institute

About the Bell Institute:

The Alexander Graham Bell Institute (The Bell Institute) of the Cape Breton University was incorporated on September 13, 1977. It is directed by a Board of Trustees representing the Bell family, Cape Breton University and members of the community. Over the years, the Bell institute has achieved several notable milestones including consolidating photographs, personal notes, and technical work of Alexander Graham Bell, completing a comprehensive index of these holdings, and conducting scholarly study of these materials.

The Bell Institute is dedicated to the memory of Dr. Alexander Graham Bell and his work. Continued study of Dr. Bell's work ("Mining for nuggets") and development of new applied research projects are motivated by a desire to continue his high standard of principle, his practical spirit and his social conscience.

The Alexander Graham Bell family collection brings together a wide range of documents accumulated by Dr. Bell and his family during their time in Baddeck, Nova Scotia. The Alexander Graham Bell institute has developed a comprehensive index of these materials. This index, with online access to several components of the Bell collection, can be accessed using the World Wide Web.

The **Alexander Graham Bell Institute** of Cape Breton University houses the archives of the work the inventor did while he was in Baddeck, Nova Scotia. Click on "holdings" to find links to this archival collection.

Access this Web site from http://www.myreportlinks.com

they kept improving their hydrofoils, and in 1919, their HD-4 hydrofoil set a world speed record of 71 miles (114 kilometers) per hour.

➲A Lasting Achievement

Regardless of everything else Bell accomplished in his wonderful life, we remember him for the telephone. And, the fact is, life as we know it today would not be possible had the telephone never been invented. We take for granted the power to communicate almost instantly with people anywhere in the world. Cell phones have only magnified that ability. And the latest phones allow us to do more than just speak. We can take photos,

▲ *With or without a hydrofoil, the busy inventor enjoyed spending time on—or in—the water.*

connect to the Internet, listen to music, and play computer games. None of this would have been possible without the amazing achievements of Alexander Graham Bell, the genius behind the telephone.

A TELECOMMUNICATIONS EXPERIMENT

To help you understand how a telephone works, build your own. You will need two paper cups, some string, and a partner.

MATERIALS:

- **two large paper cups**
- **non-stretchable thread or kite string**
- **Scotch tape**
- **scissors**
- **sewing needle**

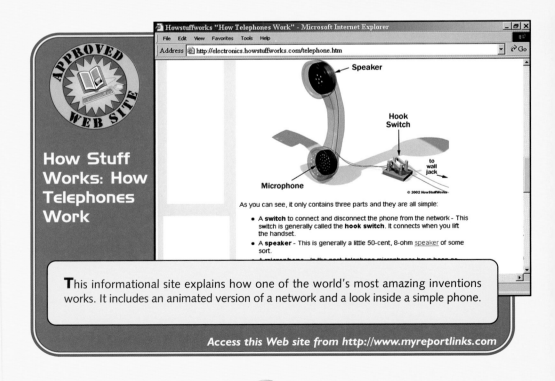

How Stuff Works: How Telephones Work

This informational site explains how one of the world's most amazing inventions works. It includes an animated version of a network and a look inside a simple phone.

Access this Web site from http://www.myreportlinks.com

Punch a tiny hole in the center of the bottom of each cup with a sewing needle.

Cut a piece of string about 100 feet (30 meters) long.

Pull one end of the string through the bottom of one cup.

Knot or tape the string so it cannot go back through the hole when the string is pulled tight.

Repeat Steps 3 and 4 with the other cup and the other end of the string.

Each person takes a cup and moves apart until the string is tight.

One person talks into one of the cups while the other person holds the other cup to his or her ear.

The person listening should be able to hear what the other person says.

How the Two-Cups-and-a-String "Phone" Works

When one person talks into his or her cup, the bottom of the cup acts as a diaphragm. It vibrates with the sound waves. It actually moves back and forth one thousand-or-more times per second with the sound waves of the speaker's voice. The vibrations travel through the string by pulling the string back and forth. This causes the bottom of the second cup, which also acts as a diaphragm, to vibrate back and forth just like the first cup is vibrating. This produces sound waves that can be

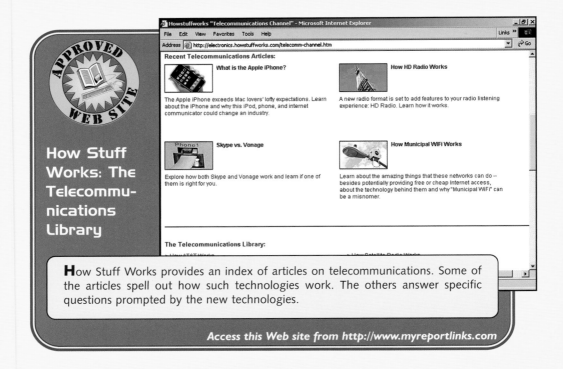

How Stuff Works: The Telecommunications Library

Howstuffworks "Telecommunications Channel" - Microsoft Internet Explorer

File   Edit   View   Favorites   Tools   Help

Address http://electronics.howstuffworks.com/telecomm-channel.htm

Recent Telecommunications Articles:

What is the Apple iPhone?

The Apple iPhone exceeds Mac lovers' lofty expectations. Learn about the iPhone and why this iPod, phone, and internet communicator could change an industry.

How HD Radio Works

A new radio format is set to add features to your radio listening experience: HD Radio. Learn how it works.

Skype vs. Vonage

Explore how both Skype and Vonage work and learn if one of them is right for you.

How Municipal WiFi Works

Learn about the amazing things that these networks can do -- besides potentially providing free or cheap Internet access, about the technology behind them and why "Municipal WiFi" can be a misnomer.

The Telecommunications Library:

How Stuff Works provides an index of articles on telecommunications. Some of the articles spell out how such technologies work. The others answer specific questions prompted by the new technologies.

Access this Web site from http://www.myreportlinks.com

heard by the second person. And this is how the second person can hear what the first person says.

→How a Telephone Works

A real telephone works in much the same way as the two-cups-and-a-string phone. But in a real telephone, electric current replaces the string. Sound waves of the person speaking cause vibrations in a thin metal diaphragm in the transmitter. The vibrations rapidly compress and uncompress carbon granules, changing their resistance. A current of electricity passing through the granules is strengthened or lessened by the changing resistance. At the other end, the rapidly changing electric current reaching the receiver runs through a speaker and causes its metal diaphragm to vibrate back and forth. These vibrations create sound waves that are transmitted to the ear. This is how the second person hears the first person speaking.

Report Links

The Internet sites described below can be accessed at
http://www.myreportlinks.com

▶**The Alexander Graham Bell Family Papers at the Library of Congress**
Editor's Choice Get a feel for Alexander Graham Bell's thoughts and his era by reading his writings.

▶*American Experience:* **The Telephone**
Editor's Choice A PBS site that explores Bell and others involved in the invention of the telephone.

▶**The Case Files: Alexander Graham Bell**
Editor's Choice A science museum chronicles the development of the telephone.

▶**Alexander Graham Bell Association for the Deaf and Hard of Hearing**
Editor's Choice An organization founded by Bell continues his work with the deaf.

▶**Alexander Graham Bell (1847–1922)**
Editor's Choice Learn about Bell and Victorian-era technology.

▶**The Centennial Exhibition, Philadelphia 1876**
Editor's Choice Relive the 1876 Centennial Exhibition in Philadelphia.

▶**Ailerons**
Learn the mechanics behind Bell's contributions to aviation.

▶**Alexander Graham Bell at National Aviation Hall of Fame**
Read about Bell's accomplishments in the field of aviation.

▶**Alexander Graham Bell Institute**
A Canadian institute dedicated to Bell's memory holds a collection of his writings.

▶**Alexander Graham Bell National Historic Site of Canada**
Learn about the work Bell did while living at Baddeck, Nova Scotia, his summer home.

▶*American Heritage:* **Inventing the Telephone and Triggering All-Out Patent War**
A magazine article examines the race to patent the telephone.

▶**Bell 'did not invent telephone'**
Read about a competitor to Bell in the development of the telephone.

▶**Bell Labs**
Learn about Bell Labs, a home for technological innovation.

▶**CNN.com: Wireless Society**
Learn how far modern telecommunications technology has come since Bell's time.

▶**Edison Birthplace Museum**
Learn about Thomas Edison, a competitor to Bell in communications technology.

The Internet sites described below can be accessed at http://www.myreportlinks.com

▶**Elisha Gray**
Explore the life of Elisha Gray, an inventor who also worked to develop the telephone.

▶**Gardiner Greene Hubbard**
Bell's influential father-in-law is profiled.

▶**History of the U.S. Telegraph Industry**
Read about the rise and fall of the telegraph in American history.

▶**How Stuff Works: How Telephones Work**
Learn how a telephone works from this informational site.

▶**How Stuff Works: The Telecommunications Library**
Learn about modern telecommunications technology.

▶**Lasers and Fiber Optics**
Read about fiber optics and its role in advanced telecommunications.

▶**Samuel Morse/Morse Code**
Read about the creator of Morse code.

▶***The Story of My Life* by Helen Keller**
Read a digital version of Helen Keller's life story.

▶**Telecommunications Virtual Museum**
Visit an online museum of telecommunications technology.

▶**The Telegraph Office**
Use this Web site to learn about wireless telegraphy.

▶**Telephone**
Learn more about the development of telecommunications in the twentieth century.

▶**The Telephone History Web site**
A history of telephones is presented by this site.

▶**Thomas A. Watson**
Learn about the man who assisted Bell in developing the telephone.

▶**Transistorized! Alexander Graham Bell**
A PBS site offers a brief history of the life of Bell.

▶**Visible Speech**
See the visible speech system developed by Bell's father.

aileron—A hinged section on the trailing edge of an airplane wing that controls the plane's rolling movements.

anatomy—The science of the structure of the body, learned by dissection (cutting up) of cadavers, or dead bodies.

audiometer—A machine that tests a person's hearing.

aviation—The operation of heavier-than-air aircraft.

caveat—The right to file for a patent at a later date. Caveats were confidential declarations made by inventors for devices that were not yet ready to be patented.

circuit—The path of electric current.

deaf-mute—A person who cannot hear or speak.

diaphragm—A thin flexible disk that vibrates when struck by sound waves.

electrodynamic—Powered by the interactions of electric currents with magnets.

electromagnet—A core of magnetic material surrounded by a coil of wire through which an electric current is passed to magnetize the core.

elocution—The art of public speaking.

exchange—A central office where telephone lines are connected, allowing communication.

hearing tube—A horn-shaped instrument that directs sounds to the user's ear.

hydrofoil—A boat which, at speed, rises out of the water supported on winglike struts, or *foils,* that project from the lower hull.

improvise—To make something up on the spot such as music or lines in a play.

iron lung—A metal breathing machine that encloses the whole body except for the head and provides artificial respiration for those with severe breathing difficulties.

Morse code—A system of sending messages by a series of dots and dashes for letters.

patent—An official document that prevents others from copying an inventor's invention and marketing it as their own.

receiver—The part of the telephone one presses to the ear.

subsidiary—A company owned and controlled by another company.

switchboard—A panel on which electric switches are mounted, allowing current to be controlled and moved. Switchboard operators controlled these switches to make telephone transmission possible.

telegraphy—A system for sending long-distance messages by electric current.

tetrahedron—A four-sided shape with three triangles forming a pyramid, with a fourth triangle forming the bottom.

transmitter—The part of the telephone one holds near the mouth.

tuberculosis—An infectious lung disease caused by bacterial infection.

tuning fork—A two-pronged tool that vibrates at a certain pitch when struck.

Chapter 1. Communication Before the Invention of the Telephone

1. James L Roark, Michael P. Johnson, Patricia Cline Cohen, Sarah Stage, Alan Lawson, and Susan M. Hartmann, *The American Promise: A History of the United States*, vol. 1 (Boston: Bedford/St. Martin's, 2002), p. 375.

2. Ibid.

Chapter 2. Alexander Graham Bell: The Early Years

1. Edwin S. Grosvenor and Morgan Wesson, *Alexander Graham Bell: The Life and Times of the Man Who Invented the Telephone* (New York: Harry N. Abrams, Inc., 1997), p. 15.

2. The Alexander Graham Bell Papers at the Library of Congress, "Letter from Alexander Graham Bell to Mabel Hubbard Bell, December 6, 1876," *The Library of Congress, Manuscript Division,* n.d., <http://memory.loc.gov /ammem/bellhtml/bellhome.html> (February 28, 2007).

3. Grosvenor and Wesson, p. 17.

4. The Alexander Graham Bell Papers at the Library of Congress, Notes of Early Life, "My First Invention," Article by Alexander Graham Bell, 1910, *The Library of Congress, Manuscript Division,* n.d., <http://memory.loc.gov/ammem /bellhtml/bellhome.html> (February 28, 2007).

5. Ibid.

6. Ibid.

7. The Alexander Graham Bell Papers at the Library of Congress, Notes of Early Life, "Teaching a Dog to Talk," Article by Alexander Graham Bell, 1910, *The Library of Congress, Manuscript Division,* n.d., <http://memory.loc.gov /ammem/bellhtml/bellhome.html> (February 28, 2007).

8. Robert V. Bruce, *Bell: Alexander Graham Bell and the Conquest of Solitude* (Boston: Little, Brown and Company, 1973), p. 28.

9. Ibid., p. 34.

10. Grosvenor and Wesson, p. 23.

11. Ibid.

12. Ibid., p. 30.

Chapter 3. Experiments With Telegraphy

1. Thomas B. Costain, *The Chord of Steel: The Story of the Invention of the Telephone* (New York: Doubleday & Company, Inc., 1960), p. 72.

2. Edwin S. Grosvenor and Morgan Wesson, *Alexander Graham Bell: The Life and Times of the Man Who Invented the Telephone* (New York: Harry N. Abrams, Inc., 1997), p. 36.

Chapter 4. Inventing the Telephone

1. Edwin S. Grosvenor and Morgan Wesson, *Alexander Graham Bell: The Life and Times of the Man Who Invented the Telephone* (New York: Harry N. Abrams, Inc., 1997), p. 44.

2. Ibid.

3. The Alexander Graham Bell Papers at the Library of Congress, "Letter from Alexander Graham Bell to Alexander Melville Bell, Eliza Symonds Bell, Carrie Bell, November 23, 1874," *The Library of Congress, Manuscript Division,* n.d., <http://memory.loc.gov/ammem/bellhtml/bellhome.html> (February 28, 2007).

4. Ibid.

5. Thomas B. Costain, *The Chord of Steel: The Story of the Invention of the Telephone* (New York: Doubleday & Company, Inc., 1960), p. 149.

6. Ibid., p. 150.

7. Ibid., p. 151.

8. Ibid., p. 152.

9. Grosvenor and Wesson, p. 62.

10. Ibid., p. 63.

11. Ibid., p. 64.

12. Robert V. Bruce, *Bell: Alexander Graham Bell and the Conquest of Solitude* (Boston: Little, Brown and Company, 1973), p. 181.

13. Ibid.

Chapter 5. How the Telephone Changed the World

1. Robert V. Bruce, *Bell: Alexander Graham Bell and the Conquest of Solitude* (Boston: Little, Brown and Company, 1973), p. 255.

2. Edwin S. Grosvenor and Morgan Wesson, *Alexander Graham Bell: The Life and Times of the Man Who Invented the Telephone* (New York: Harry N. Abrams, Inc., 1997), p. 121.

3. The American Experience: Program Description, "The Telephone," *PBS,* n.d., <http://www.pbs.org/wgbh/amex/telephone/filmmore/description.html> (February 23, 2007).

4. Grosvenor and Wesson, p. 86.

5. Ibid., pp. 243, 246.

6. Ibid., p. 246.

Chapter 6. Bell's Other Inventions

1. Lemelson Center for the Study of Invention and Innovation, "Invention at Play: Alexander Graham Bell, Telephone Inventor," *Smithsonian National Museum of American History,* n.d., <http://inventionatplay.org/inventors_bel.html> (October 26, 2006).

2. IP Mall Resources, "Quotes on Patent Lawyers—compiled by Homer Blair," *Franklin Pierce Law Center,* n.d., <http://ipmall.info/hosted_resources/blair_quotes.asp> (February 22, 2007).

3. Dorothy Harley Eber, *Genius at Work: Images of Alexander Graham Bell* (New York: The Viking Press, 1982), p. 71.

4. John Albert Macy, *The Story of My Life by Helen Keller, With Her Letters (1887–1901) and a Supplementary Account of Her Education, Including Passages From the Reports and Letters of Her Teacher, Anne Mansfield Sullivan,* e-text can be found online at *Project Gutenberg,* n.d., <http://www.gutenberg.org/dirs/etext00/kelle10.txt> (October 24, 2006).

5. Robert V. Bruce, *Bell: Alexander Graham Bell and the Conquest of Solitude* (Boston: Little, Brown and Company, 1973), p. 406.

6. Judith St. George, *Dear Dr. Bell...Your Friend, Helen Keller* (New York: G. P. Putman's Sons, 1992), p. 68.

7. Ibid., p. 77.

8. Robert V. Bruce, *Bell: Alexander Graham Bell and the Conquest of Solitude* (Boston: Little, Brown and Company, 1973), p. 337.

Bankston, John. *Alexander Graham Bell and the Story of the Telephone.* Hockessin, Del.: Mitchell Lane Publishers, 2005.

Dash, Joan. *The World at Her Fingertips: The Story of Helen Keller.* New York: Scholastic Press, 2001.

Gains, Ann. *Alexander Graham Bell.* Vero Beach, Fla.: Rourke Books, 2002.

Ganeri, Anita. *Alexander Graham Bell.* London: Thameside Press, 2000.

Haven, Kendall. *Alexander Graham Bell: Inventor and Visionary.* New York: Franklin Watts, 2003.

Hegedus, Alannah, and Kaitlin Rainey. *Bleeps and Blips to Rocket Ships: Great Inventions in Communications.* Toronto: Tundra Books, 2001.

Mathews, Tom. *Always Inventing: A Photobiography of Alexander Graham Bell.* Washington, D.C.: National Geographic Society, 1999.

McCormick, Anita Louise. *The Invention of the Telegraph and Telephone in American History.* Berkeley Heights, N.J.: Enslow Publishers, 2004.

Platt, Richard. *Eureka! Great Inventions and How They Happened.* Boston: Kingfisher, 2003.

Pollard, Michael. *Alexander Graham Bell: Father of Modern Communication.* Woodbridge, Conn.: Blackbirch Press, 2000.

Stefoff, Rebecca. *The Telephone.* New York: Marshall Cavendish Benchmark, 2006.

A

A. G. Bell Association for the
Deaf, 95
Aerial Experiment Association,
110, 111
formation of, 7
ailerons, 110, 111
American Civil War, 15–17
American Telephone and
Telegraph Company (AT&T)
89
Ampere, André, 13
audiometer, 6, 99

B

Baldwin, Casey, 111
Battle of New Orleans, 9
Beinn Bhreagh, 83, 85
Bell, Alexander Graham
birth of, 6, 20
death of, 7, 92
education of, 26–29
family life, 20–21
as inventor, 94
Keller, Helen and, 95–98
legacy, 19, 92–93, 112–113
marriage of, 6, 47, 82
as musician, 27–28
sounds, fascination with,
21–24
wheat husking process, 29–30
Bell, Alexander (grandfather),
23, 30, 37
Bell, Alexander Melville, 20,
23–25, 30, 35, 39–41. See
also Visible Speech system.
Bell, Edward, 20, 37
Bell, Eliza Grace, 24, 25, 27
Bell, Melville, 20, 31–35, 38
Bell Patent Association, 6, 51–54
Bell Telephone Company
formation of, 6, 83–86
growth of, 88–90
patent lawsuits, 86–88
bel unit, 6, 99
Berliner, Emile, 88
Bertini, Auguste Benoit, 27, 28

Blake, Clarence J., 51, 53
Boston School for Deaf-Mutes, 6,
41–42
Bourseul, Charles, 60–61
Buchanan, James, 17

C

Canada, relocation to, 6, 39–40
carbon transmitter, 87–88
Centennial Exhibition, 6, 78–81
Clarke School for the Deaf, 46
communication
pre-telephone, 8–9
teaching, as private tutor,
42–44
Cooke, William Fothergill, 10

D

deafness, causes of, 25
decibels, 99
Dom Pedro,
Emperor of Brazil, 81

E

ears, function of, 24–26
Edison, Thomas, 54, 62, 63,
86–88
electromagnetism, 13

F

fiber optics, 100–102
Field, Cyrus, 16–17
flight experiments, 7, 107–111
Forlanini, Enrico, 111

G

Garfield, James, 103–106
Gray, Elisha
caveat filed by, 74
patent lawsuit by, 86
photograph of, 55
in telephone race, 54, 62–64
Western Union support of, 45
Great Eastern, 17
Grosvenor, Gilbert H., 6–7

H

harmonic telegraph, 44–49, 54,
61–63, 68. See also
telegraph.

Helmholtz, Hermann von, 37
Henry, Joseph, 13
Hubbard, Gardiner Greene
    employment of Bell as tutor,
        46, 48
    harmonic telegraph support
        by, 53–54, 68
    telephone demonstration and,
        79–80
    telephone patent filing by,
        73–74
Hubbard, Mabel
    on AG Bell, 83
    as AG Bell's student, 46
    courtship of, 70–73
    marriage of, 6, 47, 82
    photograph, 47
hydrofoil boats, 7, 111–112

I

inventions
    audiometer, 6, 99
    flight experiments, 7,
        107–111
    hydrofoil boats, 7, 111–112
    metal detector, 6, 103–106
    phonautograph, 6, 49–51
    photophone, 6, 99–103
    vacuum jacket respirator, 6,
        106–109
iron lungs, 107

J

Jackson, Andrew, 9

K

Keller, Helen, 95–98

L

Langley, Samuel, 110
lasers, 100–102
Lincoln, Abraham, 15
London School for the Deaf,
    6, 38
London years, 6, 30–38

M

manned flight experiments, 7,
    107–111

mechanical speaking machine,
    31–35
metal detector, 6, 103–106
Meucci, Antonio, 59–60
Morse, Samuel F. B., 10–12. See
    also telegraph.
Morse code, 11–13, 19,
    45–46, 64

N

National Geographic Magazine,
    6–7
National Geographic Society,
    6–7, 48

O

operators, 88

P

patent defined, 12–13
patent grants
    lawsuits, 86–88
    telegraph, 12–13
    telephone, 6, 73–75, 87
phonautograph, 6, 49–51
photophone, 6, 99–103

R

railroads, 15
Reis, Johann Philipp, 61, 86

S

Sanders, George, 42–44, 46
Sanders, Thomas, 42, 51–54, 73
selenium cells, 99
Silver Dart, 7, 107–111
sound experiments
    quality, improvement of,
        86–87
    tuning forks, 36–37, 45–46
    vowel sounds, 37
Stearns, Joseph B., 45
switchboards, 88

T

teaching positions
    Boston School for Deaf-
        Mutes, 6, 41–42
    Clarke School for the
        Deaf, 46

London School for the Deaf,
6, 38
as private tutor, 42–44, 46,
95–98
Weston House Academy, 6,
35–37
telegraph
applications of, 13–15
benefits of, 15–16
duplex, 45
globalization and, 16–18
harmonic, 44–49, 54,
61–63, 68
invention of, 9–13
limitations of, 18–19
patent grant, 12–13
talking, 54–55
telephone
activity, 114–117
benefits of, 19, 92–93,
112–113
breakthrough, 66–68
coast-to-coast conversation, 7,
90–92
demonstrations of, 6, 60,
78–81
early experiments, 63–66, 70
evolution of, 87–88
history of, 57–63
notes, first transmission of,
6, 66
patent grants, 6, 73–75, 87
sketches, 67, 77
sound quality, improvement
of, 86–87
theory, 56–57, 60–63,
115–117
transatlantic conversation, 92
words, first transmission of,
6, 76–78
telephone directories, 88
telephone exchanges, 88
Thomson, William, 81
tuning fork experiments, 36–37,
45–46
Twain, Mark, 88–89

U
undulatory current, 66

V
vacuum jacket respirator, 6,
106–109
Vail, Alfred, 11
Victoria, Queen, 17, 82
Visible Speech system
Centennial Exhibition
display of, 80
demonstration of, 41, 81
described, 35, 36
invention of, 24, 25
teaching, use of in, 6, 38,
41, 80
voice, transmission of
Bell's interest in, 46
issues in, 63–66, 86–88
Meucci, 59
photophone, 102–103
Reis, 61
Volta, Alessandro, 13
Volta Laboratory, 94
vowel sounds experiments, 37

W
War of 1812, 9
Watson, Thomas, 7, 48–49, 50,
63–68, 76–78, 87
Western Union Telegraph
Company, 45, 60, 64, 83
Weston House Academy, 6, 35–37
wheat husking process, 29–30
Wheatstone, Charles, 10, 31
Wright brothers, 11